second edition

THE Human Side
of High
Performance

Empowering
Yourself for
the FUTURE

KENDALL/HUNT PUBLISHING COMPANY
4050 Westmark Drive   Dubuque, Iowa 52002

Cover image © 1999 by PhotoDisc.

Library of Congress Catalog Card Number: 99-67136

Printed in the United States of America
10   9   8

To my late father, Richard, who told me I could do anything I wanted to do, and my mother, Helen, who made darn sure I got it done!

To my wife Dr. Judy for having the capacity to balance me. Finally, to my three sons Benjamin, Nicholas, and Jeffrey, for bringing true joy into my life!

Contents

Steve Wiley is a colorful business entrepreneur with a magnetic personality. His energetic public speaking style affects audience members in a very positive way. This is because Steve has a refreshing and humorous method of communicating and a personal exuberance that has captivated and enlightened hundreds of corporate clients. Frequently, audience members ask him what secret recipe he eats for breakfast! Here is someone so good at his craft that audience members are drawn to him as when watching a prodigy perform. They enjoy listening for the sheer excellence of his craft on display.

Now, for the first time in book form, Steve has compiled his best and most exciting ideas about personal and professional effectiveness. There may no one surefire formula that leads to success in our business lives, but Steve believes that people extend the most consideration to people they like. He demonstrates that we can make ourselves more likable when we release from within us a special quality that adds sparkle to our interactions with co-workers, customers and everyone else.

The insights Steve brings you between the covers of his book may change your professional results and give a boost to your personal life as well. *The Human Side of High Performance* is about much more than increasing your sales, becoming a more productive worker or achieving top efficiency in a managerial or technical job. It is about those things, but also about a special brand of enthusiasm and sense of purpose that can bring us truly magical consequences.

· *Acknowledgments*

*F*irst and foremost I would like to thank my special friend Gary Lowenthal, "the head bean his self" whose friendship, mentoring, sense of humor, and monumental business success, have not only inspired me like nothing else, but have helped me through some pretty tough times. My friendship with Bob Monahan has also supported me through thick and thin for nearly thirty years. I would like to also thank my very talented friend Ritch Shydner for contributing the comedic twist to my work, and Don Rinehart whose illustrations added those elements that words sometimes cannot capture. I would also like to thank my friends at the Pritikin Longevity Centers who have impacted not only my life, but the lives of over 70,000 participants.

Special acknowledgment goes to Dr. Joseph Crowley, who along with Kendall/Hunt, had the patience with me to get this project done.

*I*t's really a privilege to think of you reading this book, since it is my first. The concept of someone reading my words instead of listening to me talk is somewhat different for me. I do not know anything about you and I cannot see you to gauge your reaction. This bothered me at first, so I did a little research and I found a study done at Harvard University in 1989 about readers of business books. The study determined that while the book was open, one-third of the readers will be thinking of a past sexual encounter. It went on to say that another third of the readers will be thinking about a future sexual encounter! Fortunately for me, at least one-third of the readers would actually concentrate on the words on the page. This study gives me great comfort, because I know that regardless of how poorly I have written this book, two-thirds of you are going to have a good time!

It bothers me a little that I have no way of knowing whether you will be reading this in your office or your home, or under what conditions you will approach it. You may be pressed for time, or feeling relaxed and open to the message it contains. Whatever frame of mind you are in, you are the one person whose needs count the most to me right now, and I can assure you that this book was designed to allow you to take it a piece at a time, at your own pace. Some of the most important parts of the book require you to take a written test. I hope you will do so at a suitable time and place, so that the maximum benefits of this information can be yours. So, as you sit comfortably in your reading environment, let's move into the subject area. I'm so excited about your joining me that I can't wait for us to begin!

I haven't done many impressive things in my life. In fact, the only thing I've done that may be interesting—not impressive but interesting—was back in high school a long time ago. I went to Bowie High School in Prince George's County, Maryland, with a girl named Kathy Epstein. Not very interesting . . . not very impressive, you're thinking. But what is interesting is she grew up to be Kathy Lee Gifford. So I've got to tell you when you go to high school with someone who becomes pretty famous, it seriously alters your recollection of that friendship. It works like this: the more famous that person becomes, the tighter you can remember being.

I doubt that she knows me from a hole in the ground, but after she began doing some local television, people would say, "Hey, Steve, didn't you go out with Kathy Epstein?" and I'd say, "Yeah, we dated." And then she moved up to regional television and her popularity widened. People from my high-school class would say, "Didn't you go out with Kathy Epstein?" And I'd say, "Oh, yes, we were tight for a couple of years!" Then she started doing network television every day and exploded into megastardom. And the few people that remembered we had gone out would say, "Whatever happened between you and Kathy Lee? You dated, didn't you?" I'd say, "Yeah, she was a very nice person, and we did spend some time together. But I finally had to dump her. She was a very nice person but we were in high school and I was broke. Friday night would come along and I'd want to get a sandwich or go to the movies. But no, she wanted to go on a four-, seven- or nine-day cruise; I just couldn't afford it."

Finally, I need to tell you on a serious note, she's bitter about that to this day. Have you seen her on television recently? She's singing, "If you could see me now." That's directed toward me, I know it! If the truth must be known, the real reason it did not work out with Kathy Lee is that I realized early on I could never be "frank" with her!

Chapter One

Ain't No Mountain High Enough

*And when you have reached the mountain top,
then you shall begin to climb.*

—Kahlil Gibran

I frequently give a presentation called "The Human Side of High Performance." I've had the privilege of delivering it to some of the finest organizations in the world. Whether I present it for sales and marketing audiences or executives for such great organizations as Pfizer Pharmaceuticals, the Gannett Companies, IBM and Ford Motor Company, the ingredients of the talk are generally the same.

Once last year I had the United States Secret Service as a client. That outfit has some interesting challenges. For example, they told me of a time when President Clinton and his wife wanted to go back to Little Rock, but the family did not want to travel on Air Force One. It was a vacation, so they wanted to drive. They rented a nondescript rental car and drove to Little Rock. This was quite a challenge to the Secret Service, which had about fifteen vehicles in the entourage: motorcycles, vans, jeeps, and so forth. On the outskirts of Little Rock, the President and his wife had to stop at a service station to use the restroom. And so the walkie talkies were chattering and the protective people were anxious about such an unprecedented thing. Bill went into the restroom and ran back to the car. Hillary went into the restroom, but instead of coming back to the car she walked up to the attendant and gave him a little kiss on the cheek, and a hug, and then returned to the car. And Bill said, "What the heck was that all about?" She said, "I dated that guy in high school, I hadn't seen him in years!" So as the car drove off, Bill got that smug look on his face and he said,

Ain't no Mountain High Enough.

"Just think, Hillary, if you had married him, today you'd be the wife of a gas station attendant." She said, "No, no, Bill, if I had married him, today he'd be President!"

So I give presentations on high performance and get paid well for doing so. But I didn't just wake up one day and decide I wanted to talk to people, to help people be more productive and more effective as sales or business professionals. In fact, let me give you a little bit of my history, how I got to where I'm doing this for a living. It began by trying to help myself. Then it led to helping other people. In the 1980s, I started a company with six hundred bucks. I took six hundred dollars and started a company in Gettysburg, Pennsylvania. We went into the exterior restoration of historic structures: beautiful brick, marble, granite buildings. And what we would do is restore these treasured buildings back to their historic, pristine nature. On the whole it went pretty well because there are a lot of historic buildings in Gettysburg to restore. So my associates and I, observing that this business was ticking, decided to open up another office in Pittsburgh. That business flourished, so we opened up another in Richmond. The next thing you know I owned the fastest growing franchise in North America, with 130 offices in three countries. I raised millions and millions of dollars in venture capital and was on the front cover of *Entrepreneur,* the front cover of *Inc.* magazine, a featured story in *USA Today's* Money Section. Life was good! That is, until 1989, when all of a sudden my little company *lost* 4.7 million dollars. Think about that for a second. It wasn't my family's company, it wasn't the company I just happened to work for. It was the company I had started from scratch with six hundred dollars. And in 1989 it lost 4.7 million dollars.

So you can say that in 1989, pretty much my full-time job was to lose money. I would leave the house in the morning and say, "See you, sweetheart. I'm going to go lose some money. Be back about six." And when you're losing four hundred thousand dollars a month you can't pay a lot of your large bills. And when you can't pay your large bills, the people to whom you owe a lot of money, say several hundred thousand dollars

a piece, don't go to collection agencies. They go to see an attorney. And what does the attorney suggest they do? Sue. So in 1989 I had sixteen major litigations going on in eleven states and two countries. I had sixteen sets of my own attorneys, just to help me survive this litigation. Now when you can't pay your big bills, obviously you can't pay your little bills either. Altogether I had millions of dollars in unpaid bills. Some creditors then began to go to collection agencies. I had 387 accounts go to collection. Now, I don't know if you ever had one bill go to collection because you couldn't pay it, didn't want to pay it or refused to pay it. Collection agencies and lawyers make your life miserable.

Multiply that misery by sixteen litigations and 387 collection agencies. Also, in 1989, February 11, a day I won't soon forget, the IRS came in and said they'd like to have a look

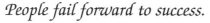

People fail forward to success.

—Mary Kay Ash

around. And so they started what they called a TCA, a total company audit. Two agents told me we needed to go over a few things. Then those same agents came to my office every day, five days a week for six and a half months. After that length of time, the IRS demanded a quarter million dollars in additional taxes from the corporation, and eighty-seven dollars from me. I couldn't for the life of me decipher what the U.S. government was going to do with my eighty-seven dollars. It was during the time of peak activity for the space shuttle, so I used to have a vision of a Cape Canaveral countdown going, "10-9-8-7 . . . Wiley's check in yet? Hold off the launch! Hold it off." Eighty-seven bucks, think of it. In 1989 I also had four root canals, so it wasn't a particularly good year. So I woke up one day and I thought to myself, I've got to make a couple of changes if I'm going to survive.

I thought to myself, I've got to get better at selling. I must become a world-class salesman. I've got to become more effective at selling myself, my expertise, my products and my services. I had better improve my plan to get out of trouble with these creditors. I also have to become a more effective leader. But before I could get better at selling and become a more effective leader, I had to get well. Because you see, I was fifty pounds overweight and taking two kinds of blood pressure medication. My blood pressure was still 180 over 115 on a good day, and I know you understand the significance of blood pressure numbers like those.

So I decided I needed to get myself well. It's just like when you get on a commercial airline and the safety crew has that announcement, "In the event of an emergency, if you're traveling with a small child (or a business associate that is acting like a small child), please put the oxygen mask on yourself first, then the small child." I have three little boys, and the first time I heard the announcement, I thought, "That doesn't make any sense. I have three little boys and we're in an emergency situation. There's no oxygen; the mask comes down in front of me; I'm going to want to put it on them first." Why would the airline ask me to put it on myself first? Because I'd be unable to help anybody else if I passed out. It's the same thing I'm talking about here. I had to get well in order to help myself regain control over my business affairs.

As a little side note on airlines, they don't do this anymore, but several years ago, they also used to announce, "In the event of an emergency, remove all sharp objects from your pockets." I thought, here I am on a jumbo jet, going six hundred miles per hour into the side of a mountain. I've got a number two lead pencil in my pocket. What do you think the cause of death is going to be? Lead poisoning? I don't think so. Boom! Impact is what gets you every time!

Anyway, back to the matter at hand. Is it important to be a better leader, more effective at selling and able to produce more? Sure it is! It's very important. But I wonder if we realize just how important it is. A study was done of six thousand purchasers of products and services. Not a survey, but a study. There's a difference. I can show you a survey telling you that a large number of persons who own books such as this never read them. It's as if they buy them to put them on a shelf and hope they learn something by osmosis.

A study is a little more scientific. Thousands of purchasers of high-ticket business items were asked, "What specifically do you buy when you make a purchase?" They came back with three responses. They said, we buy the company, we buy the product and we buy the sales representative. Then further studies showed which one of these three things is most important. One asked why people would stop doing business with a supplier. Two-thirds of them said it was not price, not quality, but a breakdown in communication with the company. Who's in charge of communication at your company? Are you starting to feel a little self-conscious? Who's in charge of communication? You should feel a little bit of recognition there, because *you* are in charge of communication.

Now let's go over this one more time.

- Eight-six percent of the people said they buy because of the sales representative.
- Fully two-thirds of the people who stopped doing business with a company said they stopped because of a breakdown in communication.

It wasn't price, it wasn't quality. It was a breakdown in communication. That's pretty powerful. Think about it. Here you work for a large company with an incredible wealth of resources. You've got all this research and development, training and years of experience with the company, all the resources, people, product, services and time. All this wonderful corporate energy and a tremendous, almost unlimited, resource base. Your potential territory for selling is virtually unlimited—the world. Potential customers are everyone and anyone who can use your products, your services or solutions. So you have these immense resources and this incredible potential market. How are the two connected? Through this little tiny line, and it's called the sales representative. So I suggest to you that becoming more empowered, learning how to be more productive, selling more effectively and becoming a more effective leader is not only important, it's absolutely essential for personal, professional and company survival.

There is a lot of weight on our shoulders as representatives of our company. So let's talk about increasing our own productivity—the results we get. To do so we've got to become more effective at this thing we call selling. How are you doing at this thing called selling? Take the pressure off yourself as an individual for a moment and let me ask you—how are we as a nation doing at selling? Are Americans pretty effective sales professionals? My friend, we as Americans are probably the least effective salespeople on the planet. I don't say that to insult anyone, just to reflect on it. It is troubling. *Selling* magazine reported in an article about a year ago that "people in . . . industry are light years behind when it comes to the ability and effectiveness in selling." So when I make a presentation to an American company, I ask them how can it be that we as Americans—corporate Americans—are the least effective sales professionals on the planet? Why? Does that make any sense?

Why should we be especially ineffective at selling? The main answer seems to come out of the recent past—after World War II, when we were the only industrial country left standing intact. Think about it, an American company came up with a great product, spent enough money on advertising, and *boom,* you had a successful car, *boom,* you had a successful pill. Whatever the product may have been, it was a success. If it was dog food, there was always a dog out there to buy it. In that environment, Americans could afford the luxury of being order takers. Just be at the right place at the right time and make your quota.

This is no longer the case, because now we have competition, serious competition, throughout the globe. Purchasing agents have fiscal responsibility. Customers want to hear from your CFO what your internal costs are. We no longer can afford the luxury of just being order takers. Welcome to the new millennium.

> *In summary . . .*
> - *You can make yourself a success.*
> - *You are in charge of your own communications.*

Success is not the result of spontaneous combustion. You must set yourself on fire.
                                        —*Reggie Leach*

You are not here merely to make a living. You are here to enable the world to live more amply, with greater vision, and with a finer spirit of hope and achievement. You are here to enrich the world. You impoverish yourself if you forget this errand.

—Woodrow Wilson

Chapter Two

We're "Bad at Sell" and We're Not Gonna Take It Anymore

*I*t's not our fault that the pace of life and our own competitive natures turn us into aggressive maniacs. I mean, who has time to be patient anymore? The word "patient" itself reminds me of a skit that a good friend of mine, who is a comedian, does about selling in America. He will parody a situation like this. "Oh, my appendix burst! Sweetheart, get the car keys; we'll go compare a few emergency room prices." They go to the emergency room. He says, "My appendix burst. How much do you charge for an appendectomy?"

"Sixty-six hundred dollars."

"Okay, that's a little steep, I'm going to get a few other prices. What time do you close tonight? I might be back."

Well obviously, this is a comedy routine. In real life you aren't about to haggle with a hospital. You're strapped to a gurney and it is plain that either they operate on your ruptured appendix or you die of internal poisoning. Hospitals get used to dictating the terms of the arrangement to patients who are horizontal at the time they apply for admission.

Well, welcome to "managed care."

Unless you work in a hospital—and under today's new health coverages, even if you do work in a hospital—most of your customers are not without alternatives. We are in a competitive era when customers ask relentless questions about price, and even delve into our cost structure and inquire about organizational efficiencies before deciding whether to award us their business.

American companies no longer can afford the luxury of planning simply to be at the right place at the right time, any more than an individual representative can just answer the phone all day hoping someone calls in with an order sooner or later. But as a cultural observation, we never really had to be effective as sales professionals during the past couple of generations. There are other cultural reasons why Americans still might be at the bottom of the list when it comes to effective selling. Think about what traits we have that are not conducive to selling. Let me ask you this question. Are we very patient? Are we patient as a culture? No, we're impatient. When do we want results? Now! Instant gratification! Yesterday would be even better! Is that conducive to cultivating long-term relationships? Of course not.

Because of the hectic pace of modern life, or because of the sheer variety of options available at any one time, we have become incredibly impatient. When you make a cross-cultural comparison with other world cultures, we in America probably have the least patience on the planet. Patience isn't even regarded as a virtue in this country, although it is highly respected in other cultures, especially in Asia and the Middle East. I don't think western Europeans are significantly more patient than we are, just possibly more charming—the French may kiss you on both cheeks, while stepping on your foot, for example. In this country we have a low level of patience in our general dealings with each other. Then, when you cull from all Americans the people who *sell* in America, that group is even less patient. Then you go to one more level: the difference between men and women.

If you're a man in sales in America today you are the most impatient creature on God's earth. And if you don't believe that and you are a guy, think about the last time you rode in an automobile as a passenger when a woman was driving. I can hear you now. "Run the light, run the light, run the light, ahhh, you could've made it! Ahh, that truck wasn't that big. Now we have to sit here for a whole minute! Damn! If only I hadn't lost my license."

We are categorically impatient. When you and I want to conclude a deal yesterday, that's not conducive to a sale. Nor is it going to help build any sort of relationship with the client. Because we want to get in there, score and get out. If that's not bad enough, another reason why we sales professionals may not be effective as we should is that we're extremely competitive! Would you agree with that? When we enter into an interaction with anybody we're almost obsessed with winning. If you don't believe me, go to a five-year-old's tee ball game and look into the stands at the parents. The mommies and daddies are not just cheering. It's "Nicholas, you strike out one more time and you don't eat next week!"

On a more serious level, my wife, who is a psychologist, will tell you that our competitive instinct—or more specifically the win-lose motivation, or what she calls a zero-sum transaction—is expressed at the level of ego. And ego may be the real enemy here. Because ego is one side of a two-headed coin whose opposite side is *fear.* Fear of losing. Fear of looking bad. Fear of rejection, whatever. The best definition I ever heard of "fear" was to make it into an acronym, F-E-A-R, standing for False Expectations About Reality. Our cave-dwelling ancestors survived on the fight-or-flee instinct, and although mercantile society has evolved for over five hundred years well beyond the point where a competitive business transaction involves life-or-death stakes, we are individually not always as enlightened. In plain English, we feel at the level of ego that we have to win, we have to make the score, we have to sell, we have to move the product, we have to triumph over the customer's resistance, even if it means shoving the product down his or her throat.

Recently, USA Today published the results of a poll in which a thousand people chosen at random were asked to name their favorite movie actor. The newspaper then announced the top ten winners. Perhaps it was the phrasing of the question, but no female actors landed in the top ten. Most of the names on the top-ten list were predictable enough—DeNiro, Nicholson, Newman, Ford, and so on, but guess who was number one? And not by a little—but by a very wide margin? John Wayne! Imagine, John Wayne, who is of course no longer living, and who hasn't made a movie in twenty-five years, was number one by a huge margin. That speaks volumes about our culture, I believe.

Here you have the busy sales professional, imbued with the American cultural influence, which includes a heavy dose of John Wayne movies, also maybe feeling a little insecure one day because of being behind on quota, making a call on a prospective customer. It's fight or flight. The prospect has actually become an enemy in terms of psychological transference. So the sales rep plays hardball and metaphorically beats the customer to a pulp, landing a lopsided deal that will look great back at the office.

But wait—if I just beat you to a pulp today, what's going to happen tomorrow? If I forced you to buy today, what's going to happen in the future? Either you will refuse to see me or you'll spend the rest of your life trying to get back at me. Selling, as engaging in battle, aggravated by impatience and the ego-fueled competitive instinct, fails miserably. Patience is a virtue. It always has been, and always will be. Competitiveness may be fine on a football field, but when it translates to a zero-sum, "if you win therefore I lose" mentality, it will sabotage results.

It is quite possible, and always desirable, for both parties in a business transaction—or any other human interaction—to come away winners. When one party comes away missing a face that's been ripped off, how will that contribute to the renewal of a positive business relationship over the long term? Obviously it won't—if anything it will start a cycle of injury, revenge, retaliation and ultimately the loss of an opportunity to do more business. Checking your ego at the customer's door and leaving the win-lose mentality behind allows you to pay more attention to what your customer needs and wants, for much better results. Later in the book, I will give you a technique for doing this. I call it "Listen Until It Hurts."

Patience can be called the forgotten virtue in America. It goes hand in glove with another undervalued character builder beginning with the letter "p"—persistence. There is a wealth of documentation on the power of persistence. All other things being equal, the patient, persistent individual will succeed over the jackrabbit, competitive, hardball player virtually every time. Let's just say that persistence can't be fully realized without patience. So, here we are, culturally impatient and prone to behave on the ego plane, the dimension where one must win and one must lose, the zero sum arena. We have no choice but to pay attention to the consequences of these actions and to change these traits at the level where they do the most damage: within our own heads.

⟫◆⟪

Often times the only difference between screaming success and mediocrity is just an additional five minutes of perseverance.

—Steven B. Wiley

⟫◆⟪

The competitive nature of our companies' business has changed and will continue to change in the next millennium. The bad news is that we're not really effective at selling, given our cultural and psychological baggage, and the fact that sales training in America concentrates on the wrong thing. The good news is that we can change it. We said earlier that two-thirds of the people who stop doing business with your company do so because of a breakdown in communication. Now here are the startling results of a study done years ago by Xerox Corporation and never refuted since.

- Only 7 percent of communication is *what* you say: features and benefits, reasons to buy, any other technical information about the company.

- Thirty-eight percent of communication is *how* you say it: the tone of your voice, your attitude and demeanor (these are big factors).

- Fifty-five percent of communication is *physiology:* your posture, your facial expression, your body language.

Wow! Ninety-three percent of communication has nothing to do with features and benefits. So I urge you to concentrate on that 93 percent. This will profoundly affect your ability to get your way—possibly for the first time. I'm not saying you should ignore the 7 percent, the features and benefits part of communication. But knowing those is the price of admission. You wouldn't be reading this book if you didn't know the features and benefits of your products or services. Isn't that right? Put it this way, if you don't know the features and benefits of your products or services, you should put down this book and read some feature and benefit literature instead. That's the price of admission. You don't need me to help you understand how your own business products work. But maybe I can help you with the other 93 percent of communication, which is by far the most important.

Selling has a standard definition: fulfilling a need. I'd like you to consider broadening the definition to include consultative selling. In one sentence: you become an effective consultative sales professional when you cease being a salesperson and you commence being a resource person. I want you to make the transition from sales professional to resource professional. I'd like you to have business cards that say Resource Professional. And the sooner you make the transition, the better off you'll be for your own personal future and for the future of your organization.

To be a resource person, you need to begin with a mission statement. When I give a presentation and ask, "How many in the audience have a mission statement?" often not one hand in the room goes up. These aren't small rooms, either. I have spoken before audiences at large companies. The organizations themselves all have mission statements. Ford Motor Company has a wonderful mission statement, IBM has an incredible mission statement. Reebok has a pretty neat mission statement; Brigg's has one, too. Every company that I work for has a mission statement. But the sales professionals, the resource professionals of the company don't have their own personal mission statements. That's the problem. So if you don't have one, you are not alone.

Once someone raised his hand when I asked who had a mission statement. I said, "That's great! What's your mission statement?" The person answered, "To make more money." This is not the proper approach.

I had to grow up a lot before I matured to the point where I had a mission statement I thought was worthy. My mission statement is to provide the most powerful sales training in the world, and to do so in an entertaining way. I want to have a profound impact on each and every individual in each and every audience—to make heroes of people who decide to have me speak to their companies, and world-class resource people of the audience. That's basically my mission statement. It may sound grandiose but think about it for yourself. Instead of your mission statement being expressed as "to make a hundred calls today," or "to make more money this month than last month," why don't you try a mission statement that says, "I'm going to make my client a hero. I'm going to solve my client's problem.

I'm going to make my client a hero at his or her organization today." That's a worthy mission for you.

When you stretch yourself a bit and think of your mission statement as more global, as encompassing other people, it works wonders. It may sound corny, but as soon as I began concentrating on having a profound impact on audiences and making heroes out of the people who brought me into their organizations, things began to click for me. You can get equal or better results by having a mission statement that is more focused on how your work can be a benefit to other people. This means that it's not appropriate for your mission statement to be making more money, but to make heroes of the people you deal with. You're going to make friends with the people you deal with. You're going to enter into partnerships with the people you deal with. That's the pinnacle of empowerment.

Later on, when I show you how to construct a mission statement, I'd like you to resolve to work on it. I will give you a technique to write a personal mission statement in one sentence and never forget what it is.

In summary . . .

- *Practice patience.*
- *Both parties as winners.*
- *Watch your body language.*
- *Follow your personal mission statement.*

Chapter Three

Look in the Mirror without a Flinch

Have patience with all things, but chiefly have patience with yourself. Do not lose courage in considering your own imperfections but instantly set about remedying them—every day begin the task anew.

—Saint Francis de Sales

Knowledge of personal styles—your own and your customer's—is a core competency of great value to you. In the last chapter I used the term "features and benefits," referring to your knowledge of your company's products and services as the price of admission. You've simply got to know them thoroughly, I said. Now I'd like you to concentrate on your own personal features and benefits. Let's tally what distinctive assets we have as individuals. Let's think of these as the features and benefits of our own personalities.

You may have heard of the Myers Briggs Type Indicator, sometimes called the Myers Briggs test. It's a psychological profile that reveals what kind of personality type you exhibit.

It does this by placing you in one of sixteen possible groups of personalities. Then you learn to estimate where other people would fit into these categories. So that's sixteen possible categories for you, sixteen possible categories for your client. This is supposed to help you identify communication strategies. The problem I have with Myers Briggs when I'm acting as a sales professional is that first of all, here I have all these features and benefits of my products and services to remember. Then I have my sixteen possible personalities. Then the sixteen possible personalities my client could have. This adds up to 256 combinations, and I walk into the client's place of business wondering which of them I'll run into. Talk about sensory overload! This is permutation overload.

Another thing about Myers Briggs is that it confirms what type of fundamental personality you have. And guess what? You can't change your fundamental personality throughout your lifetime. Well, it may be possible, but it isn't likely. A problem with Myers Briggs is that we give the indicator to a thousand salespeople, and after they take the test, they conclude they have the wrong personality. This is nonsense, because whatever personality type you are, you can achieve world-class stature in selling. Whether your personality is reserved or outgoing, it doesn't matter. Embrace your fundamental personality; just know that there are different types out there, and resolve to do a better job of relating to them.

As my wife, who is a psychologist would tell you, my personality and yours are a product of parental expectations, rules, socioeconomic status and lots of other diverse influences. Our personality is how we choose to reveal ourselves to the external world. Strike up a conversation with a fellow passenger on a plane or a train, and pay attention to how that person describes himself or herself. People usually define themselves in terms of roles. "I am the purchasing manager for Acme Corporation," or "I am a sales professional temporarily working for Acme Corporation while preparing for something better to come along." Or "I'm a young mother juggling the demands of career, home and children." In other words, they describe them-

Which One?

selves with references to externalities. Or they say, "I'm a real friendly, outgoing type." Or "I'm kind of reserved and very thoughtful." All of these are descriptions of oneself using a point of view drawn from external references.

Personality type is pretty much a given, but you can modify your personality *style*. What if I asked you to make ten new friends today? How would you go about it? What if you had a goal to enter into five new partnerships this week? To help you in this area, I've included with the book a written instrument called the Insight Inventory. The Insight Inventory, which I'll ask you to self-administer in a few minutes, is going to analyze your style in four areas. These are the areas that I think matter when it comes to effectively communicating with people.

- The first area we're going to analyze is how you get your way—directly or indirectly or somewhere in between. And it's important for you to know. It doesn't matter if you're direct or indirect, but it's important for you to know which area you are in.

- Then we're going to find out how you respond to people. You're either very outgoing or reserved, or in between. What matters is that you know how you come across.

- The third area has to do with how you pace activity. You either have a sense of urgency—got to get it done yesterday—or you're very steady—you ponder and compare and contrast. Either way is perfectly acceptable. It is just important to know which style you lean toward.

- And the final area, we want to know how it is you manage details. Are you precise? You've got to computerize, categorize and alphabetize. Or are you completely unstructured? Where's my hat? Has anyone seen my keys? Whether precise or loosey goosey, the only thing that matters is that you know what tendency you have.

So instead of having you fret over sixteen personality types, we're going to find out what your style is when it comes to these four areas.

How do you get your way, compared to how your customer gets his or her way? Are you direct or indirect? How do you respond to people? Are you outgoing or reserved? How do you manage your time? How do you pace activity? Is it with a sense of urgency, or do you deliberate, compare and contrast? Finally, how do you handle details? Are you precise and systematic? Or are you unstructured and chaotic? You need to know that before you get up in the morning, because if you're calling someone who is unstructured and you are highly structured, or you wish to visit someone who is reserved and you're outgoing, or you go to a customer who wanted everything done yesterday, and you want to compare and contrast for five minutes, it will be like speaking two different languages.

Always remember since you are in charge of communication, and since 93 percent of communication has nothing to do with features and benefits, it's vital to find out what style you have and how it will match or conflict with the style of the person you are dealing with. It's professional suicide if you don't know personal styles.

Let me give you an example of the benefits of becoming aware of your own style and personal communication preference. My wife and I took the test you're about to undergo. My wife, Judy, Dr. Wiley (she has a Ph.D. in psychology—in fact she's been analyzing me ever since we got married, which has been a long, tough project for her), took this test with me. It only took us seven minutes to take the test and seven minutes to correct it, but it served as the best marriage counseling we've ever had. I'm talking about maybe two years of counseling in fourteen minutes. We found out we're on opposite ends of the chart in every one of these categories. I'm direct; she's indirect. I'm outgoing; she's reserved. I have a sense of urgency; she likes to contrast and compare. She handles details magnificently; I don't know where my shoes are!

I'm very direct; she's indirect. I'll be watching TV, and she'll come down and say, "Steve, we're out of toilet paper." Five minutes goes by and she'll say, "Steve, did you hear me? We're out of toilet paper." Now does she mean we're out of toilet paper? No, she means go get some toilet paper. Now I'm a little more direct. When I say, "We're out of toilet paper," I mean we're out of toilet paper! You're on your way to the bathroom? You better grab a newspaper because we're out of toilet paper.

When it comes to pacing activity, I'm a wreck, I've got to get it done yesterday. I have this constant sense of urgency. She likes to contrast and compare. It took me fifteen years of marriage to realize that when my wife says, "Let's go looking for a couch this weekend," we might not find a couch. When I go looking for a couch, I'm going to buy it, bag it and drag it back. So although we're on opposite ends of the chart, by learning to stretch our styles, life has improved for us both!

Every client that you meet approaches these four categories with a different style. And yet our tendency is to conduct ourselves in the same manner all day long.

The Insight Inventory begins on page 29 of this book. It's pretty much self-explanatory, but I'd like to give you a few tips that will help you through it. When you open up the Insight Inventory, there's a work style and a personal style questionnaire, numbered 1 through 32. First, answer the questions under work style. Handle these questions with the thought that this is how you conduct yourself at work. For instance, number 2 is "talkative." If you're not very talkative, check 1; if you're somewhat talkative, check 2, if you're pretty talkative, check 3; if you can't keep your mouth shut, check 4. Then, after you do 1 through 32 in work style, go to personal style. Check numbers 1 through 32, but this time answer the questions as they relate to how you conduct yourself at home. The test is self correcting, so you will be able to get instant scoring feedback and a graph of your own style once you take this test.

Turn to page 36 and take the test now.

Once the test is corrected, you will get four scores. For example, you may be *very direct, very outgoing, very urgent* and *very precise.* You will have a description of your style.

Of course we're going to want to know the description of your clients' style. Sometimes I'm asked, "How do I know what their style is? I took the test, they didn't!" I say shame on you if you don't take the time to get to know your own clients to find out whether they're more outgoing than reserved; more precise or unstructured. We're not talking about selling vacuum cleaners door-to-door. We're talking about cultivating relationships.

Pages 31, 32, 33, and 34 of the Insight Inventory pretty much walk you through the steps you need for this exercise to be meaningful. Once you have the scores for *Work Style* and *Personal Style,* just read through the description of *How You Get Your Way* on page 31 and be sure to look at your style opposite—to see how they get their way. Notice the stark differences? Now look at page 33, which demonstrates what kind of situations cause you stress. My favorite example is of an Urgent type dealing with a Steady type. Slow decision-making drives the Urgent type up a wall, while pressure to hurry a decision causes the Steady person to balk. It's a classic, almost comical situation, if it were not so true to life.

The next page puts it all together, by giving you some pointed hints on how to achieve better communications by flexing—that means temporarily changing—your style into something more suited to other person. What this does is help other people, your customers, co-workers, friends and family members, relate to you and like you more. Why? Because they will find you easier to be around, that's why.

I'd like to share with you some of the comparative results I get in my audiences. I'll ask, how many in the audience came out more direct than indirect on the personal style? Half the hands will go up. Then I'll ask, "How many of you came up more reserved than outgoing when it comes to responding to people?" Half the people will raise their hands. With every question I ask, approximately half the audience is always on one side of the continuum and half on the other. Do you see what I mean when I say we might have to stretch our style four, five, six or ten times a day? Because I've never had an audience turn out to be entirely direct or indirect. And yet we tend to go through our day making the same style of presentation. Obviously, this should change.

Did you notice you had a different work style than a personal style? People often do, which is further evidence that we can adapt our style. We conduct ourselves differently at home than we do at work. You may want to conduct yourself differently on the second call than you did on the first call. The third call you may want to stretch your style again. You don't have to change your personality! Embrace your personality—just stretch your style. To assist you in doing this, Step 7 in the Insight Inventory is very valuable. It says, for example, that if you are an indirect person, and you wish to better communicate with a direct individual, you should be a little more assertive. You may want to avoid appearing unsure, hesitant or tentative. "Directs" will misinterpret this as meaning you just don't have the knowledge you should. If you are a Direct dealing with an Indirect, you may want to avoid coming across as too self assured or having too many strong convictions. Indirects may read this as arrogance.

If you're outgoing, you might want to be sensitive to the reserved person's need for quiet time. If you're a Reserved dealing with an Outgoing, you may want to be a little enthusiastic or animated in talking. Otherwise they may misinterpret your reserve as a lack of interest. Please keep this Insight Inventory available. You'll find it to be a valuable resource when it comes to dealing with different styles of people.

There are different things you can do to stretch your style. My wife and I are a perfect example of how you can improve communication. For an Urgent to better communicate with a Steady, you may want to be more patient. Don't push. Give advance notice. If you're a Steady dealing with an Urgent, you may want to make decisions more quickly, or at least let them know you are thinking about it. Present your ideas quickly and succinctly and be ready to take action.

If you're an Unstructured and you want to better communicate with a Precise, you should be on time for the meeting and be as organized as possible. You should get your facts and details together before trying to persuade a Precise. If you're a Precise and you're dealing with an Unstructured, be sure your comments contribute to the primary topic or goal. Don't bring up too many details. Don't try to enforce too many rules too quickly. Avoid excessive perfectionism.

Just for fun, think of a very difficult customer, or a very difficult human being with whom you have to interact. Use the back of the Insight Inventory and chart what you think their style might be. Are they direct or indirect? Are they reserved or outgoing? Are they reserved or steady? Are they unstructured or precise? And then put some time and effort into thinking about how you may want to conduct yourself to more successfully interact and communicate with that person. I call this the "difficult customer exercise."

Please use the Insight Inventory as a resource to measure your style and connect with someone at the level of their style. It's all part of waking up in the morning to the understanding that we should be resource people instead of salespeople. We need to have our own personal mission statement. We know the kind of assets we have. We know how to adapt our style so that it synergizes with someone else's, someone important. Someone like our customer!

INSIGHT
Inventory®
... understanding yourself and others

Improving Personal Effectiveness

The Insight Inventory® test begins on page 36. Before you complete the test, please make note of these instructions.

On page 36, put a "✓" next to each of the numbered adjectives indicating how much they describe your Work Style and Personal Style.

After you complete page 36, turn to the Scoring Sheet on page 37. To find your results, transcribe the "✓" you chose for each adjective in the test onto the same position on the scoring sheet. Be sure to place the "✓" in the exact position on the line. Then, look at the point value that appears in your choice box and copy that point value to the box at the right of the line.

Once you have transcribed the point values, add up the points in each of the four vertical columns and enter the sums into the large blocks labeled A, B, C, and D, at the bottom of page 37.

Step 1 Take out the INSIGHT Inventory questionnaire, read the instructions for completing it, and begin. When you are finished, tear off the first sheet and follow the scoring instructions on the second sheet.

Step 2 Transfer your Work and Personal Style results to this page by writing your scores in the boxes to the left (labled A, B, C & D). Next chart these scores on the graphs below.

Example
Work Style

Personal Style

Work Style Scores

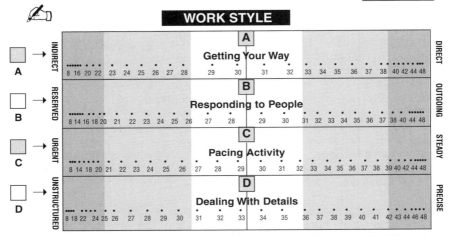

WORK STYLE

A — INDIRECT / DIRECT
Getting Your Way
8 16 20 22 23 24 25 26 27 28 29 30 31 32 33 34 35 36 37 38 40 42 44 48

B — RESERVED / OUTGOING
Responding to People
8 14 16 18 20 21 22 23 24 25 26 27 28 29 30 31 32 33 34 35 36 37 38 40 44 48

C — URGENT / STEADY
Pacing Activity
8 14 18 20 21 22 23 24 25 26 27 28 29 30 31 32 33 34 35 36 37 38 39 40 42 44 48

D — UNSTRUCTURED / PRECISE
Dealing With Details
8 18 22 24 25 26 27 28 29 30 31 32 33 34 35 36 37 38 39 40 41 42 43 44 46 48

Your Work Style indicates how you behave at work. A number of factors influence your Work Style such as deadlines, the nature of your job, relationships with coworkers, and your manager's leadership style.

Personal Style Scores

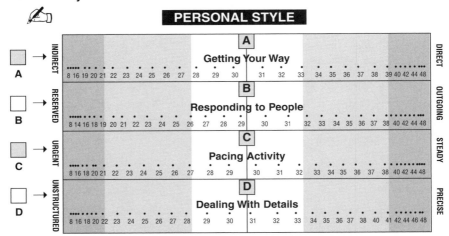

PERSONAL STYLE

A — INDIRECT / DIRECT
Getting Your Way
8 16 19 20 21 22 23 24 25 26 27 28 29 30 31 32 33 34 35 36 37 38 39 40 42 44 48

B — RESERVED / OUTGOING
Responding to People
8 14 16 18 19 20 21 22 23 24 25 26 27 28 29 30 31 32 33 34 35 36 37 38 40 42 44 48

C — URGENT / STEADY
Pacing Activity
8 16 18 20 21 22 23 24 25 26 27 28 29 30 31 32 33 34 35 36 37 38 40 42 44 48

D — UNSTRUCTURED / PRECISE
Dealing With Details
8 16 18 20 22 23 24 25 26 27 28 29 30 31 32 33 34 35 36 37 38 40 41 42 44 46 48

Your Personal Style indicates how you behave away from work. A number of factors influence your Personal Style such as responsibilities at home, relationships with family members, and social activities with friends.

© 1988—revised 1995, Patrick G. Handley, Ph.D.

Step 3

Notice the various levels of shade intensity and where your score falls on each scale. This will help you identify how closely the descriptions of each style fit you.

8 16 20 22   23   24   25   26   27   28   29   30 | 31   32   33   34   35   36   37   38   40 42 44 48

No shade
If your score falls in the area with no shade, some characteristics from both styles on the left and right sides of the center line may describe you.

Light shade
If your score falls in the light shaded area, many characteristics of that style may be descriptive of you. A few characteristics from the style on the other side may also fit.

Dark shade
If your score falls in the dark shaded area, most of the characteristics of the style on that side will describe you.

Identifying your style descriptions

Step 4

Circle your style on each of the four scales (A, B, C, & D) from your Work Style profile. Then, read the descriptive phrases under that style and check (✔) the ones that best describe you at work. This helps you identify the descriptions that fit you on each scale. *(It may be helpful to repeat this activity later on your Personal Style using "✘"s rather than checks.)*

Example:

OUTGOING

You respond to others in a talkative, expressive manner.
You:
__ Prefer interacting with lots of people and groups and enjoy attention from others
✔ Express feelings readily and openly
__ Get energized by people contact and lots of activity
✔ Prefer to talk problems out to clarify your feelings
✔ Share thoughts and feelings openly with friends and new acquaintances
__ Use lots of gestures and facial expressions when you talk

A

INDIRECT

Getting Your Way
How you influence others and assert yourself

DIRECT

You influence others using strategy and diplomacy.
You:
__ Lead through a supportive and tactful manner
__ Project an air of modesty, often dismissing achievements
__ Come across as approachable and nonintimidating
__ Resolve conflicts through diplomacy and harmony
__ Prefer to negotiate rather than to argue or debate
__ State your thoughts carefully and diplomatically
__ Tend to "ask" rather than "tell"

You influence others using assertiveness and conviction.
You:
__ Lead through a take-charge and straightforward manner
__ Project an air of self-confidence and accomplishment
__ Come across as forceful and intimidating at times
__ Resolve conflicts by directly confronting issues
__ Openly argue or debate your points of view or opinions
__ State your thoughts candidly and frankly
__ Tend to "tell" rather than "ask"

B

RESERVED

Responding to People
How you approach and respond to others, particularly groups

OUTGOING

You respond to others in a quiet, reserved manner.
You:
__ Prefer to interact with others one on one or in small groups and avoid attention when possible
__ Hold back expression of feelings in a self-contained style
__ Get energized when alone and away from activity
__ Prefer to think problems through to clarify your feelings
__ Share thoughts and feelings with only a few people you know well
__ Use few gestures and facial expressions when you talk

You respond to others in a talkative, expressive manner.
You:
__ Prefer interacting with lots of people and groups and enjoy attention from others
__ Express feelings readily and openly
__ Get energized by people contact and lots of activity
__ Prefer to talk problems out to clarify your feelings
__ Share thoughts and feelings openly with friends and new acquaintances
__ Use lots of gestures and facial expressions when you talk

© 1988—revised 1995, Patrick G. Handley, Ph.D.

| URGENT | **Pacing Activity** How you take action and make decisions | STEADY |

You take action and make decisions quickly.
You:
__ Consider a few important options before deciding
__ Like change, variety, action
__ Get things done by encouraging change
__ Make most decisions quickly—"Opportunity knocks once"
__ Prefer short-term projects requiring quick responses
__ Burn energy in a fast-paced, sporadic manner
__ React quickly when frustrated and angered

You take action and make decisions after much deliberation.
You:
__ Consider many options and alternatives before deciding
__ Like consistency and stability
__ Get things done through perseverance and persistence
__ Make most decisions cautiously—"Timing is everything"
__ Prefer long-term projects requiring calculated responses
__ Burn energy in an even-paced, very consistent manner
__ React slowly when frustrated and angered

| UNSTRUCTURED | **Dealing With Details** How you structure time, carry out projects, and handle details | PRECISE |

You strive to have time unstructured and plans flexible.
You:
__ Tend to postpone organizing and attending to details
__ Use unconventional procedures to accomplish tasks
__ Like plans open and somewhat unpredictable
__ Proceed on projects before reading all the directions
__ Take pride in doing things in different ways
__ Get frustrated by too many guidelines and rules
__ Make lists but often don't follow them

You strive to have time structured and plans defined.
You:
__ Tend to organize details in a timely and thorough fashion
__ Use established procedures to accomplish tasks
__ Like plans clearly set and somewhat predictable
__ Proceed on projects only after reading all the directions
__ Take pride in doing things in proven ways
__ Get frustrated by ambiguity and lack or specific guidelines
__ Make lists and then usually follow them

Examining the differences between your Work Style and Personal Style

Identify any differences between your Work Style and Personal Style profiles. This will help you clarify how you adapt to different influences or pressures at work and at home and will help you describe different aspects of your style to others.

Differences between your Work Style and Personal Style profiles may reflect:

- changes due to stressful demands either at work or at home,
- temporary changes due to a short-term pressure, or
- learned skills, a healthy way of flexing to get along better with others.

WORK STYLE

List the factors at work that may affect your Work Style profile.

Example: Although I prefer more STEADY style, I am very URGENT at work because of the many deadlines and emergencies I handle.

_____

_____

_____

PERSONAL STYLE

List the ways your Personal Style differs from your Work Style and what factors at home influence this.

Example: I am more DIRECT at home than at work because that style works better when parenting my two rather strong-minded teenagers.

_____

_____

_____

Step 6 Read the situations below that are often stressful for each style. Then, identify the situations that are the most stressful to you and circle the ways that you typically react. This will help you anticipate situations that may cause you stress and understand how your reactions may be related to your style characteristics.

INDIRECT	Getting Your Way	DIRECT
Stressful situations: open displays of conflict; forceful confrontation and loud arguments **Reaction:** may give in, become hesitant and unsure; may avoid conflict		**Stressful situations:** not being able to voice opinions; lack of straightforward responses from others **Reaction:** may get forceful and abrupt; may get argumentative

RESERVED	Responding to People	OUTGOING
Stressful situations: group pressure to talk or share personal information; being the center of attention **Reaction:** may withdraw; may become quiet and private		**Stressful situations:** lack of people contact; loss of affirmation and group support **Reaction:** may get very talkative; may try too hard to gain approval

URGENT	Pacing Activity	STEADY
Stressful situations: lack of action; slow decision-making; changes in decisions which cause delays **Reaction:** may get frustrated and impatient; may decide too quickly		**Stressful situations:** pressure to make fast decisions; last minute deadlines; frequent interruptions **Reaction:** may find ways to postpone decisions; may delay taking action

UNSTRUCTURED	Dealing with Details	PRECISE
Stressful situations: too many policies and procedures; rigid enforcement of rules; lack of flexibility **Reaction:** may look for loopholes in rules; may not attend to details		**Stressful situations:** ambiguity and lack of organization; poor planning; unpredictable change **Reaction:** may get even more detailed; may resist change

Flexing your style to communicate better with opposite styles

Step 7 Review the guidelines below which describe how you can "flex your style" to communicate more effectively with people who have opposite styles. Then, check (✔) the guidelines where you would like to gain more skill. This will help you develop strategies for improving your communication skills and working better with others.

Flexing Your Style

To "flex your style" means to temporarily change your style so that others can relate to and communicate better with you.

For an **INDIRECT** to better communicate with a DIRECT

__ Be more assertive and forceful when presenting ideas
__ Demonstrate self-assurance through posture and voice tone
__ Stand your ground when a DIRECT challenges you
__ Avoid appearing unsure, hesitant, or tentative
__ Rehearse your opinions; even jot down some thoughts so you won't omit them in a discussion with a DIRECT

For a **DIRECT** to better communicate with an INDIRECT

__ Listen thoroughly first before debating or arguing
__ Watch your body language—avoid overpowering
__ Suggest and recommend; don't tell or command
__ Don't put down an INDIRECT's ideas—even if you are just joking
__ Avoid coming across too self-assured and too convicted; INDIRECT's may read this as arrogance

Scale A

For a **RESERVED** to better communicate with an OUTGOING
__ Be enthusiastic and animated when talking __ Use added facial expression and voice animation __ Open up your body language—use more eye contact, smiling, gesturing, etc. __ Don't be overly quiet, it's hard for an OUTGOING to read what your silence means __ Avoid holding back your feelings—express them

Scale B

For an **OUTGOING** to better communicate with a RESERVED
__ Listen carefully and encourage the RESERVED to talk __ Draw out the RESERVED using open-ended questions __ Avoid talking too much __ Don't come on overly friendly if a relationship isn't established; this may be read as superficial __ Be sensitive to the RESERVED person's need for quiet, alone time; don't take this personally

For an **URGENT** to better communicate with a STEADY
__ Be patient, don't push STEADYs to make too many fast decisions, give them advance notice __ Stick with tasks when working with a STEADY—persist, hang in there even if you get bored __ Hold back some of your snap decisions—a STEADY reads this as impulsivity and lacking restraint __ Discuss mutually acceptable deadlines, then let STEADYs work at their own pace

Scale C

For a **STEADY** to better communicate with an URGENT
__ Make decisions quicker or at least let URGENTs know what issues you are thinking about __ Match your actions to the quick pace and step of the URGENT __ Use fast speech and gestures to keep the attention of the URGENT __ Present your ideas quickly and succinctly and be ready to take action

For an **UNSTRUCTURED** to better communicate with a PRECISE
__ Be on time and be as organized as possible __ Get your facts and details together before trying to persuade the PRECISE, make notes if necessary __ Don't get discouraged if your ideas get criticized by a PRECISE—they may only want some small changes __ Don't let details drop between the cracks—PRECISEs see this as being unprepared

Scale D

For a **PRECISE** to better communicate with an UNSTRUCTURED
__ Be sure your comments contribute to the primary topic or goal; don't bring up too many details __ Don't try to enforce too many rules too quickly __ Avoid excessive perfectionism __ Stay open to unproven ideas and suggestions __ Don't be overly critical—the UNSTRUCTURED may stop bringing innovative ideas to you

Charting the profiles of your team members

Step 8

Chart your team members' profiles. This helps you recognize each other's contributions to the team, identify what each person finds stressful, and discover ways to work together better.

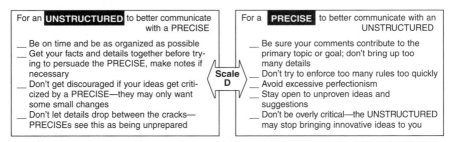

Team Leader _____ (name)

INDIRECT			DIRECT
RESERVED			OUTGOING
URGENT			STEADY
UNSTRUCTURED			PRECISE

• How this member's style contributes to the team:

_____

• What stresses this person:

_____

• How we can work together better:

_____

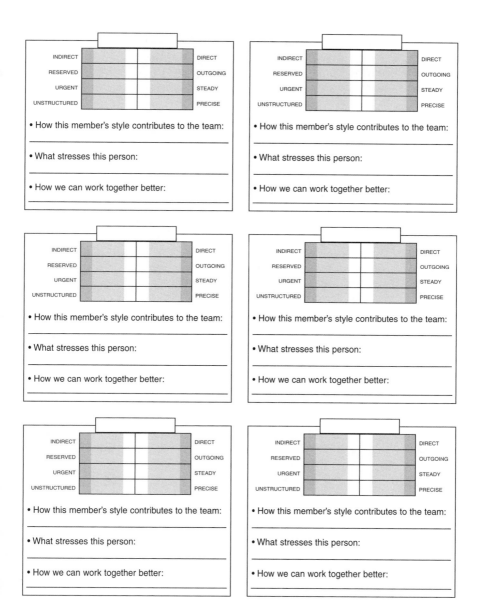

INDIRECT — DIRECT
RESERVED — OUTGOING
URGENT — STEADY
UNSTRUCTURED — PRECISE

• How this member's style contributes to the team:

• What stresses this person:

• How we can work together better:

INDIRECT — DIRECT
RESERVED — OUTGOING
URGENT — STEADY
UNSTRUCTURED — PRECISE

• How this member's style contributes to the team:

• What stresses this person:

• How we can work together better:

INDIRECT — DIRECT
RESERVED — OUTGOING
URGENT — STEADY
UNSTRUCTURED — PRECISE

• How this member's style contributes to the team:

• What stresses this person:

• How we can work together better:

INDIRECT — DIRECT
RESERVED — OUTGOING
URGENT — STEADY
UNSTRUCTURED — PRECISE

• How this member's style contributes to the team:

• What stresses this person:

• How we can work together better:

INDIRECT — DIRECT
RESERVED — OUTGOING
URGENT — STEADY
UNSTRUCTURED — PRECISE

• How this member's style contributes to the team:

• What stresses this person:

• How we can work together better:

INDIRECT — DIRECT
RESERVED — OUTGOING
URGENT — STEADY
UNSTRUCTURED — PRECISE

• How this member's style contributes to the team:

• What stresses this person:

• How we can work together better:

Make an additional copy of this page if your team has more than seven members.

INSIGHT INVENTORY® QUESTIONNAIRE

Name _____ Date _____

Instructions: Place a check in one of the blanks immediately to the right of each term as it best describes you.

not very ←→ very
descriptive   descriptive
1   2   3   4

Example: 2. Talkative . . . . ☐ ☐ ☑ ☐
3. Patient . . . . ☑ ☐ ☐ ☐

Definitions: If you are unsure about the meaning of any term, read the definitions on the back of the scoring sheet.

WORK STYLE

Check the degree to which the words in the column below are descriptive of how you believe you are most of the time at work.

not very ←→ very
descriptive   descriptive
1   2   3   4

1. Competitive. . . . . ☐ ☐ ☐ ☐
2. Talkative . . . . ☐ ☐ ☐ ☐
3. Patient . . . . ☐ ☐ ☐ ☐
4. Accurate . . . . ☐ ☐ ☐ ☐
5. Demanding . . . . ☐ ☐ ☐ ☐
6. Serene . . . . ☐ ☐ ☐ ☐
7. Animated . . . . ☐ ☐ ☐ ☐
8. Perfectionistic . . . . . . ☐ ☐ ☐ ☐
9. Domineering . . . . ☐ ☐ ☐ ☐
10. Easygoing. . . . . ☐ ☐ ☐ ☐
11. High-spirited . . . . ☐ ☐ ☐ ☐
12. Structured. . . . . ☐ ☐ ☐ ☐
13. Forceful . . . . ☐ ☐ ☐ ☐
14. Mild . . . . ☐ ☐ ☐ ☐
15. Systematic . . . . ☐ ☐ ☐ ☐
16. Convincing . . . . ☐ ☐ ☐ ☐
17. Good mixer. . . . . ☐ ☐ ☐ ☐
18. Strong-willed. . . . . . . ☐ ☐ ☐ ☐
19. Exacting . . . . ☐ ☐ ☐ ☐
20. Even-tempered . . . . . . ☐ ☐ ☐ ☐
21. Enthusiastic . . . . ☐ ☐ ☐ ☐
22. Decisive . . . . ☐ ☐ ☐ ☐
23. Detailed . . . . ☐ ☐ ☐ ☐
24. Tolerant. . . . . ☐ ☐ ☐ ☐
25. Intense . . . . ☐ ☐ ☐ ☐
26. Life of the party. . . . . . ☐ ☐ ☐ ☐
27. Daring. . . . . ☐ ☐ ☐ ☐
28. Restrained . . . . ☐ ☐ ☐ ☐
29. Particular . . . . ☐ ☐ ☐ ☐
30. Charming . . . . ☐ ☐ ☐ ☐
31. Laid-back . . . . ☐ ☐ ☐ ☐
32. Organized. . . . . ☐ ☐ ☐ ☐

PERSONAL STYLE

Some people (not all) behave differently away from work. Check the degree to which the words below describe the "at home" or personal you.

not very ←→ very
descriptive   descriptive
1   2   3   4

1. Decisive . . . . ☐ ☐ ☐ ☐
2. Enthusiastic . . . . ☐ ☐ ☐ ☐
3. Restrained . . . . ☐ ☐ ☐ ☐
4. Particular . . . . ☐ ☐ ☐ ☐
5. Intense . . . . ☐ ☐ ☐ ☐
6. Detailed . . . . ☐ ☐ ☐ ☐
7. Good mixer. . . . . ☐ ☐ ☐ ☐
8. Serene . . . . ☐ ☐ ☐ ☐
9. Accurate . . . . ☐ ☐ ☐ ☐
10. Competitive. . . . . ☐ ☐ ☐ ☐
11. Animated . . . . ☐ ☐ ☐ ☐
12. Organized. . . . . ☐ ☐ ☐ ☐
13. High-spirited . . . . ☐ ☐ ☐ ☐
14. Exacting . . . . ☐ ☐ ☐ ☐
15. Patient . . . . ☐ ☐ ☐ ☐
16. Talkative . . . . ☐ ☐ ☐ ☐
17. Easygoing. . . . . ☐ ☐ ☐ ☐
18. Forceful . . . . ☐ ☐ ☐ ☐
19. Structured. . . . . ☐ ☐ ☐ ☐
20. Life of the party. . . . . . ☐ ☐ ☐ ☐
21. Mild . . . . ☐ ☐ ☐ ☐
22. Domineering . . . . ☐ ☐ ☐ ☐
23. Systematic . . . . ☐ ☐ ☐ ☐
24. Charming . . . . ☐ ☐ ☐ ☐
25. Even-tempered . . . . . . ☐ ☐ ☐ ☐
26. Strong-willed. . . . . . . ☐ ☐ ☐ ☐
27. Perfectionistic . . . . . . ☐ ☐ ☐ ☐
28. Convincing . . . . ☐ ☐ ☐ ☐
29. Laid-back . . . . ☐ ☐ ☐ ☐
30. Demanding . . . . ☐ ☐ ☐ ☐
31. Tolerant. . . . . ☐ ☐ ☐ ☐
32. Daring. . . . . ☐ ☐ ☐ ☐

INSIGHT Inventory Scoring Sheet

| OPTIONAL | The Insight Institute, Inc. retains scores, whenever possible, for further research. To assist us please complete the following questions and return this sheet to your instructor. All information is kept confidential. *Mail to:* HRD Press, 22 Amherst Road, Amherst, MA 01002 • 1-800-822-2801 |

Name _____ Date _____ Sex _____ Company _____

Job title_____ Age _____ Race _____ Country/Nation _____

SCORING INSTRUCTIONS: Follow the two steps below to score your INSIGHT Inventory results.

① First, transfer the point value from the questionnaire to the box on the right. Follow the arrows to keep on the correct line. ──────────── **point value**

Example

② Second, add up all the points in each of the four vertical columns. Enter these sums in the large blocks—labled A, B, C, and D—located at the bottom of the page.

Follow the same procedure for scoring both the WORK STYLE and PERSONAL STYLE responses.

WORK STYLE   PERSONAL STYLE

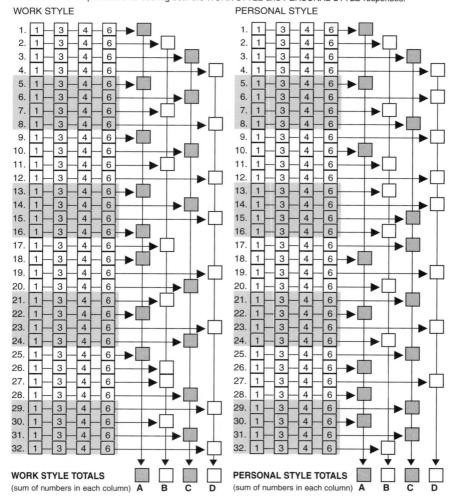

WORK STYLE TOTALS ▨ ☐ ▨ ☐
(sum of numbers in each column) **A   B   C   D**

PERSONAL STYLE TOTALS ▨ ☐ ▨ ☐
(sum of numbers in each column) **A   B   C   D**

INSIGHT INVENTORY®—EXPANDED ITEM DESCRIPTIONS

Read the definitions below if you are unclear about the meaning of any item on the inventory.

Alphabetical order:

Accurate
Attentive to details, correct, precise, puts a lot of effort into order and organization

Animated
Lively, playful, energetic, displays emotion, uses lots of facial expressions and gestures

Charming
Very friendly, talkative, gains attention when in groups of people, persuasive

Competitive
Strives to win out over others, has strong desire to have authority, enjoys debating

Convincing
Compelling, good with words, outgoing, able to influence others easily

Daring
Bold, takes risks easily, assertive, seeks adventure, nervy

Decisive
Confident, self-assured, conveys a take-charge manner, makes decisions easily

Demanding
Forceful with others, tough, will push others to do things a certain way

Detailed
Attends to small things, keeps organized, orders and plans carefully

Domineering
Enjoys being in charge, tells others what to do, straightforward, direct

Easygoing
Relaxed, patient, tolerates frustration well, steady

Enthusiastic
Shows lots of excitement, expresses feelings readily, is excitable and outgoing

Even-tempered
Not angered or frustrated easily, tolerant, mild, amiable

Exacting
Good with details, accurate, attends to every task no matter how small

Forceful
Direct, assertive, speaks candidly, vigorous, authoritative

Good mixer
Good at meeting others, makes small talk easily, warms up others quickly, expressive

High-spirited
Expresses feelings readily, animated, lively, responsive

Intense
Comes on strong, direct, forceful, fiery, self-assured

Laid-back
Calm, relaxed, steady, tolerant, not easily upset

Life of the party
Lively, expressive, meets and greets others easily, likes attention, enjoys being around lots of people

Mild
Pleasant, agreeable in nature, amiable, even-tempered

Organized
Keeps details in order, has a place for everything and keeps everything in its place

Particular
Meticulous, wants things done a certain way, careful, selective

Patient
Able to wait without getting restless, accepting, not easily upset

Perfectionist
Attends to every detail, wants things exactly right, flawless, precise

Restrained
Cautious, careful, considers many options before deciding, takes action only after much thought

Serene
Calm, easygoing, patient, able to wait without getting frustrated, not easily upset

Strong-willed
Steadfast, not easily influenced, forceful, demanding, unwaivering

Structured
Does things according to the rules, carefully follows procedure, well planned, likes systems

Systematic
Orderly, methodical, reads instructions carefully, follows the rules

Talkative
Speaks out readily in groups, expresses emotions openly, demonstrative

Tolerant
Accepting, forgives easily, lenient, patient, doesn't anger easily

---

In summary . . .

- *Evaluate yourself.*

- *Cultivate relationships.*

- *Learn to flex your personal style.*

It takes half your life before you discover life is a do-it-yourself project.

—Napoleon Hill

Chapter Four

It's the Questioning, Stupid

Listening, not imitation, may be the sincerest form of flattery.

—*Dr. Joyce Brothers*

*D*rawing out each customer's needs is the best way to discover whether you are the best one to fill them. I would like to help you turn each interaction with customers or prospects to your advantage, even when you cannot do anything for them. For that purpose, learning to ask the right questions is a far more valuable technique than explaining features and benefits. That's why "closing techniques" are a dinosaur, a relic of a bygone era. Let me explain.

There are more books on selling than there are books on self-help in the book store. The self-help section has books for women who love men too much, for women who love men who hate women, for women who love men who act like their fathers but look like their sisters. I mean they've got all kinds of books like that. Did you ever stop to think why they have so many darn books for women? Because women will buy them.

(You don't see men buying books like these. Why not? Not enough pictures, that's why.)

In the business section, there are books on start selling, stop selling, and every other kind of selling the authors can define. Most of them are based on writings from the 1920s. We're facing millennial challenges with 1920s writings and studying procedures that were developed seventy-five years ago.

I've researched hundreds of books and reviewed hundreds of tapes and the only thing that they seem to agree on is that the sales process consists of four categories. The first category is the preliminaries, you know, the introduction. The second category is the probing or the questioning. The third category is problem solving, or the features and benefits, the solutions. And the fourth category, yeah, you guessed it: the close.

Ten thousand sales professionals were asked which of those four sales categories is the most important? Do you want to guess what they guessed? You're right, the close. But they were told, yes, it's the close if you're selling vacuum cleaners door-to-door. But not when you're trying to cultivate relationships.

So their second guess was . . . ta-*da* . . . features and benefits, features and benefits; if it's not the close it must be features and benefits. But the reason features and benefits are not most important is because we get caught into a trap that way. For example, the client says, "I'd like a blue one."

We say, "We've got a red one and a green one."

"I'd like a blue one."

"We've got an orange and purple one."

"But I'd like a blue one."

"We've got a round one and a square one."

If you just lapse into this features and benefits role and you don't know what the customer wants, it's a complete waste of everyone's time. So again, the most important category of the sales process is not features and benefits.

The third guess? It must be the preliminaries. It must be the introduction. After all, you don't get a second chance to make a first impression. Yes, if you're just selling door-to-door you don't. But if you're cultivating a relationship, the duration of your sales cycle might be a week, a month or years.

It doesn't take a brain surgeon to figure out the most important category: the probe, the questions you ask. Last year corporate America spent one billion dollars—that's a thousand million dollars teaching sales professionals in North America the difference between a close-ended and an open-ended question. And you know what? It doesn't make any difference.

I want to share with you a style of questioning that's going to profoundly affect your ability to sell. But before we start talking about the most important component part of selling, the inquiry, or the probing, I've got to make sure that when you ask questions, you listen to the answers. Most of us think we're good listeners. In my case, I thought that was one of the few

things I did well until my wife set me straight. My wife said one day, "You're not a very good listener."

I said, "Judy, I have a lot of flaws, most of which you've pointed out to me, but the fact is, I listen pretty well. I'm a pretty good listener."

She said, "No, you're not."

I said, "Yes, I am."

She said "Well then, listen to this." And she read me the following paragraph.

A business person had just turned out the lights in the shop, when a man appeared and demanded money. The owner opened the cash register. The contents of the cash register were scooped up and the man sped away. A member of the police force was promptly notified.

So I said to my wife, "OK, what's your point?"

She said, "You didn't hear me."

I said, "I heard you."

She said, "But you didn't listen well."

I said, "I heard every word you said."

She said, "Just in case, I'm going to read it to you again."

So I'm going to ask you to read it again, too. I'm not going to call you stupid, but I am going to give you a hint: Read carefully.

A business person had just turned out the lights in the shop, when a man appeared and demanded money. The owner opened the cash register. The contents of the cash register were scooped up and the man sped away. A member of the police force was promptly notified.

Okay? Don't look back at this story again.

Judy said, "Answer a few questions for me." I'd like you to take out a pen or pencil and a sheet of paper to handle those questions yourself. Mark the sheet of paper with **T** for true, **F** for false, and **?** if the story doesn't tell you either way.

Here are Judy's questions.

1. A man appeared after the owner had turned off the shop lights. True, false, or unanswered in this story.
2. The robber was a man. True, false or question mark.
3. The man did not demand money. True, false or question mark.
4. The person who opened the cash register was the owner. True, false or question mark.
5. The owner scooped up the contents of the cash register and ran away. True, false or question mark.
6. Someone opened the cash register. True, false or question mark.
7. After the man who demanded money scooped up the contents of the cash register, he ran away. True, false or question mark.
8. While the cash register contained money, the story does not say how much. True, false or question mark.
9. The robber demanded money from the owner. True, false or question mark.
10. The story concerns a series of events which only refers to three people. The owner of the store, a man who demanded money and a member of the police force. True, false or question mark.

Let's find out how you did. The correct answers are

1. Question mark
2. Question mark
3. False
4. True
5. Question mark
6. True
7. Question mark

8. Question mark
9. Question mark
10. Question mark.

How did you do? Did you get them all right? Did you get nine right? Eight? Six? Well, I rest my case.

I hope this experience makes you a little more skeptical about how we pay attention. And you didn't just listen to this story, you read it—twice. For listeners it's a lot worse. In that role, our natural impatience becomes a factor. We complete people's sentences for them. We complete their thoughts for them. And we feel we know a heck of a lot more about what they want than they do. We are horrible when it comes to listening. We listen to someone speaking at 250 words a minute, yet we think a thousand words a minute. We're thinking about what we did yesterday, what we're going to do today. We think about the features and benefits of our products and services. We think about everything but what the prospect is telling us he or she wants.

My suggestion is this: **Listen Until It Hurts.** Listen until you think to yourself, "I can't listen to this person another second!" Listen until it hurts. Listening is a contact sport. You listen with your eyes. You listen with your face. You listen with your ears. You listen with your body. And you listen with a pen or pencil if necessary, and write down every word. Note taking is a flattering gesture, almost always taken as a sign of your regard for the other person's words and your determination to retain them.

Listening is a magnetic and strange thing, a creative force. The friends who listen to us are the ones we move toward. When we are listened to, it creates us, makes us unfold and expand.

—Karl Menninger

Listen till it hurts

It is imperative that we become better listeners, with a system of inquiry at our disposal. What is required is a method of probing each prospective customer. Here is a system of questioning that will profoundly improve your effectiveness as a resource person. To help you remember it (or maybe to help me remember) I call it the Wiley questioning method. The memory device is to use the letters of my surname: W-I-L-E-Y. This way, you will have a memory-link system to help employ this method. The first question will begin with W, the second with I and so on.

W—The first question you should ask in the inquiry portion of developing a partnership/friendship with clients is "What's happening in your world?" Just simply, "What's happening in your world?" You don't want to sound ignorant and walk in to a furniture factory and say, "Oh, do you make chairs here?" But make your question global in scope, a question that indicates your desire to find out what issues are affecting their business life. When you ask what's happening in their world, if they run off on a tangent about something in their personal life, so be it. Listen until it hurts. But at least ask them for a

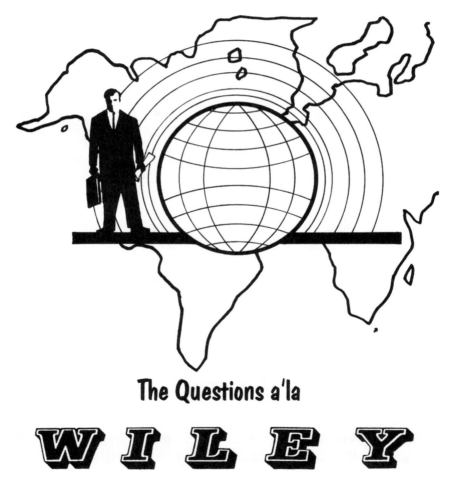

The Questions a'la

WILEY

condensed Reader's Digest description about what's going on in their world. This question has to be expansive enough so they are able to ramble on. Then listen intently to what they say, as if your life depended on it.

I—"In what areas are you having difficulty?" is the next question. If you prefer to phrase it with a more positive emphasis, then ask, "In what areas do you see the most room for improvement?" Now that you know what's going on in the customer's world, you need to discover the problem areas, those with the most room for improvement. And again, listening closely to the response is your key. Taking notes is all right; it's a signal to other parties that you are paying attention and respecting their words.

L—Third, you should say, "Let me know how these areas that need improvement are hindering your world." I understand what's going on in your world, I understand in what areas you're having difficulty. But I'd like to know how those difficult areas are affecting your world on a corporate, personal or any other level.

E—Envision. Ms. Client, Mr. Client, envision yourself wielding a magic wand. How would you fix your problem? The corollary to this question, the one you should follow up with, is "How will you recognize when it is fixed?" I mean, how many times have you solved a client's problem and the client didn't even recognize that it was fixed. You want to know up front, how is your client going to measure that the problem is fixed? What has to happen for that person to see that you have solved his or her problem?

Y—Now here is where you are going to take yourself out of the category of being a regular sales professional and into the category of becoming a world-class resource professional. I know—you're hoping that **Y** will stand for "Yes, I can help you! My solution, my product, my service is just what the doctor ordered. It chops, it slices, it dices, it's just what you want." Well, we may wish life were that easy, but the fact is that "yes I can help you with my products or services" only happens about 5 percent of the time—if you're lucky. But sales professionals typically try to force it to happen 50, 60, 70 percent of the time.

A much more effective way to handle this would be to say, "I understand what's happening in your world. I know which areas you're having difficulty in. I know what those areas of difficulty are doing to you in your world, and I know how you would fix it if you could. Yet I can't help you. I've got to be honest with you. I wish I could. But I can't help you. But I'll tell you what I am going to do. I'm going to put some time and effort into finding help for you. I used to work at another firm [or I used to work in that other field, whatever]. I think I may know where to get you help, and I am going to try to obtain that help because I want to be a resource for you."

If your product partially solves the customer's problem, then another option is "Yes, I can help you in one or two of these areas, but not all of them. So let me help you in the areas where I can and I promise you I will put time and effort into helping you get the solution for the others." Presented with a refreshing attitude like that, your clients will remember you forever. Just think about it. You helped them and it wasn't really in a self-serving capacity. You just found them help because you cared. You wanted to help them, just as you would help a friend.

As an exercise in achieving this frame of mind, sit back in your chair right now and think of a good friend. We all have a particularly cherished friend, I imagine. Envision that person right now. Think about that person; it's a pleasant thought. Now imagine the telephone rings, and it's that good friend.

"How are you doing?"

"I've got to bring my daughter to school and pick up my son, I'm really in a jam. I need a car!"

Do you think . . . hmmmmm, maybe I can rent Randy my car for sixty dollars a day? No, of course not. Do you think, maybe I can send Randy down to the local car lot and he'll buy a car and I can get a commission? Surely not. The only thing you think about is, how can I help Randy? I can lend him my car. If I can't lend him my car, maybe my sister's car is available.

If you treat your clients that way, you can cultivate the same kind of bond, the same kind of relationship, the same kind of interaction that you have with your close friend. Think of making sales calls in the manner of making a few friends today. You want to enter into a few partnerships today. So when you're asking the second question of the W-I-L-E-Y questioning series, "In what areas are you having problems?," don't be self serving and phrase it like, "In what areas are you having problems with the two-cylinder widget that I happen to sell?"

If you can be successful in questioning, or probing, in the W-I-L-E-Y manner and ask the questions as suggested, three rather magical things will happen. First, your clients, friends or partners will give you constant feedback. They'll do that because you helped them out last time—and with no personal gain. They'll remember that forever.

The second thing they'll do is recommend you passionately. You know, recommendations are still essential in business. The problem is, the days are over where three good references mean anything at all. Anybody can come up with three good references. Serial killers can come up with three good references. The fact is you want more than a reference. You want someone to *recommend you passionately.* As I sit at the keyboard typing this manuscript, I have to count on the fact that other people are recommending me passionately. While I'm in my office in Gettysburg, Pennsylvania, I have to count on the fact that someone in Seattle is talking to someone in Baltimore and saying, "You should hire Steve Wiley." And not just by saying, "Steve Wiley is a good speaker. You should have him come to your National Sales Meeting." That isn't enough!

It's really great when a company like Black & Decker recommends me to the Ford Motor Company, saying something like, "You mean to tell me you're considering Steve Wiley for your National Sales Meeting, and you haven't booked him yet? Well, you'd better hurry up or you'll miss out on a wonderful presentation, and that would really be a tragedy for your people!" Now, there's a passionate recommendation! That's the kind of recommendation you'd like to have, is it not? *That kind of recommendation makes all the difference in the world.*

Third, and here's the kicker, they will forgive you when you screw up! I don't think anyone reading this book can claim to live a life free of flaws. If you do, I'd like to know who you are. The fact is that, we're all going to screw up. And wouldn't it be great if your client not only understood, but forgave you for that!

We all make mistakes from time to time, and I can assure you I'm no exception. One time I was making a presentation, standing on a big stage with a curtain behind me. When I address a large audience I always move around quite a lot. On this particular day, I mistakenly thought that there was a wall behind the back curtain! In fact, the curtain marked the end of the platform and there was nothing behind it but air. Air—and a five-foot drop onto a concrete floor. So at a certain point in the speech, to emphasize a point I was saying, I jumped back expecting to hit the wall behind me. But when all I hit was a curtain, I began to fall backwards. Reflexively, I grabbed the curtain and held on to the fabric for a split second, probably at a forty-five degree angle, then luckily was able to pull myself upright. All this in full view of the audience. Well, they were startled at first, but after I made a few jokes about it, they willingly forgave me and gave a warm round of applause at the end of the speech.

Let me conclude this chapter with one last point about the benefit of having your client recommend you passionately. It has to do with time management—yours. When you attend a management course, one of the definitions you encounter is that management is about controlling scarce resources. The scarcest resource of all may be *time*. Time is not unlimited for any mortal human being.

There was a very expensive and extensive study commissioned by a large company in which they monitored the time management skills of the typical sales representative. This was a study of more than four hundred sales representatives, and the company wanted to know how its sales professionals spent their time. The results were incredible! Over 57 percent of the time, sales professional dealt with administrative work—filling out forms, making requests. An additional 29 percent of their time was spent traveling to and from the customer, either on an airplane, in a car or on foot. Think about those findings for a second. My goodness, if 57 percent of their time is spent doing administrative work, and 29 percent is spent going to and from customers, that leaves only 14 percent of their time to actually spend in front of their customers.

If that were not bad enough, the study found that only 25 percent of that 14 percent was spent actually speaking to the customer about purchasing something. Then the really bad news: only 10 percent of the 25 percent of the 14 percent of the time did these sales representatives receive a "yes." I don't know if you had your calculator out as you were reading this, but that comes out to less than one-half of 1 percent of the time that these sales professionals were scoring for their company.

Can a company make it on a hit ratio of 0.5 percent? This one sure didn't feel like it could. The company saw these study results and hit the panic button. It began by eliminating forms. It started to computerize more of its office operations, so its sales representatives didn't have to fill out as many forms, or mail as many forms or be on the telephone as long. The company mounted a tremendous effort and in so doing knocked that 57 percent administrative work time down to about 51 percent. Turning to the 29 percent travel time, it reorganized territories. The company got out the maps and reconfigured the entire sales effort geographically throughout the country. So it knocked the 29 percent down to 21 percent. Then they did the math: This only improved the hit ratio by about 0.25 percent. Can we increase sales by boosting the time we spend in front of the customer? Well, yes, but it is limited by intractable natural obstacles.

Think about this for a solution: What if you had some of your customer friends, your partners, recommending you passionately. Wouldn't that be great? Look at me, if I had to count on being in Boston, being in Des Moines, being in San Francisco saying, "May I speak for you?" I wouldn't have any business.

The best way for you to expand the pie is to have so many friends, and so many partners out there that someone recommending you passionately all the time!

Make it happen by using the Wiley questioning method:

W—**W**hat's happening in your world?

I—**I**n what areas are you having most difficulty, or in what areas is there most room for improvement?

L—**L**et me know what those difficult areas are doing to your world. And how are they affecting your world? I want to know because I care.

E—**E**nvision you had a magic wand and you could fix it. How would you fix it? And more importantly, how are you going to know when it is fixed?

Y—**Y**es, I can fix this part, but I can't fix the other part. But I'll tell you what I'm going to do: I'm going to try to get you that help. I'm going to put in my time and effort and be a resource for you.

In summary . . .

- *Ask the right questions—the WILEY technique.*
- *Listen til it hurts!*
- *Under-promise and over-deliver.*
- *Enter into partnerships with your clients—don't just service them.*

54

Opportunities are often missed because we are
broadcasting when we should be listening.
                              —author unknown

Chapter Five

Mission Impossible? Naaaaw

We don't see things as they are, we see things as we are.

—Anais Nin

<hr>

*T*he inscription on the Temple at Delphi admonished visitors to "Know Thyself." The master psychologist Carl Jung observed that to "know ourselves" may be the ultimate purpose of life. Before serving as a resource to other people, there is an exercise you can work on whose payoff is more powerful than you can imagine right now. I'm talking about designing your very own mission statement.

Steven Covey's ground-breaking book, *First Things First*, uses the adjective "empowering" to describe a proper, personal mission statement. He says an empowering mission statement represents the deepest and best that is within you. If there is anything worth pondering, reviewing, memorizing and writing into your heart and mind it will be your mission statement. I hope if you do not yet have one, you will begin to work on one while reading this chapter. I'll be giving you some methods for getting you started on your mission statement.

First, I have to tell you why I was so impressed after encountering Covey's book. The way it handles mission statements really got my attention. When the book talked about the power and the passion of a mission statement, the author suggested first developing a vision of what your life could represent. As a creative exercise, he said to visualize your 80th birthday. Try to imagine a wonderful celebration where relatives, friends and people from all walks of life come to honor

Self Exam

you. Yes, honor *you*. That's the point of the exercise. You have to visualize what each of these people would say about you, one by one: the qualities of character they would remember you for, outstanding contributions they might mention. What difference would you have made in their lives? Now you begin to get the purpose of this, don't you? This exercise can give you a tremendous insight into the potential power and passion of your life vision. Visualize your 80th birthday celebration. What an idea!

Covey's book teaches that in a sense we all have three lives that we lead. We have our public life, where we interact with other people at work or social or community events. We have our private life, where we operate out of the public eye, alone with our friends and family. And then we have our deep, inner life. This deep inner life is largely hidden, even from ourselves if we let it stay so. But it is in this deep inner life, this secret life, where we detect our life's mission. We don't invent a mission for ourselves so much as discern what it is from among our unique combinations of talents and preferences and within the specific opportunities we have been given in life. This is how we create a fire within, too, by connecting with this deep inner self.

If you had a powerful mission statement, it would tap directly into this fire within you. It would raise your confidence in what you are doing, provided that your actions were consistent with your mission. For example, if the realization of your mission statement require that you depart from the norm, do something unusual, swim upstream against the current of popular opinion, or change habits formed over a lifetime, you could do it. You would be acting on an independent willpower aided by a sense of purpose, not reacting to a trend or behaving instinctively. You would be exercising your free will as defined by yourself. You could then depart from the herd and develop self-reliance and discipline.

It is in the exercise of our free will that we become truly human. I can hear you say, "Big deal, humans can develop the will to do anything." But without the passion of vision, discipline is merely regimentation. Isn't it? Isn't it a drudgery? A white-knuckle, grit-your-teeth approach to life? Who wants that?

An empowering mission statement is one that describes your personal gifts and expresses your unique capacity to contribute to whatever it is you do in life. That's what a mission statement is all about. It's comprehensive and based on principles. It should address the physical, social, mental and spiritual dimensions of life. It deals with all of the significant roles in your life. Because what you're looking for is *balance,* in personal, family, professional and community roles. Does this sound like a tall order? Oh, and one more thing: it is written to inspire *you,* not to impress anyone else.

Once people have put the required level of effort into formulating their mission statements, reading what they have written is like standing on sacred ground. The statements reveal their important inner priorities. And the payoff for them is immediate, because truly meaningful mission statements create energy and commitment. Energy is the source of motivation. Energy is empowering. A proper mission statement can lift you up by its claws like an eagle and carry you to a distant cliff, from which you can look down and observe the exhilarating view.

Having a mission statement makes personal time management far easier too. No longer is it necessary to compile longer and longer daily to-do lists. Unless the task fits your mission, it probably shouldn't get that much priority. It's that simple.

Another author by the name of Lori Beth Jones has recently written a book called *The Path,* which is all about constructing mission statements. In *The Path,* Lori Beth Jones says a good mission statement needs only three elements. It should be no more than a single sentence long. It should be readily understood by a twelve-year-old, and you ought to be able to recite it at gunpoint! She got that last element from a story her uncle told her about World War II, when an unidentified soldier who appeared and could not state his mission could be shot. So, keep it simple and keep it memorable.

Before we go further I want you to discard two false assumptions that many people hold. First, my job is my mission. Your work may *express* your mission, but your mission is always larger than your job, because it reflects ultimately who you are as a person. Number two, I'm not important enough to have a mission. This is arrant nonsense, because everyone, no matter what or who that person is, has an impact on the universe. And if you don't believe that, go rent the movie *It's a Wonderful Life.*

If you're going to compose a mission statement, realize that it should fit you perfectly. It should fit your own consciousness of yourself. Not my view of you, not your mother's view of you, not your boss's view, not the view of your parole officer, if you have one. Nor does it have to fit the things and events that have happened to you in the past. It should be oriented by the present and point to the future. It doesn't matter about your past, anyway; the past is gone. In fact, if the past has brought problems for you, that may be the good news. It is a powerful moment indeed when you realize you are unhappy or frustrated with a life situation. Because that realization is the beginning of a conscious urge to change, develop energy and improve the situation.

The worksheet for a mission statement included in this chapter contains some open-ended questions designed to invoke your *vision* of the future the way you want it to be. In this way, you will formulate a vision statement that becomes a recruiting tool for your mission statement, because the vision pulls you naturally along the path of your mission.

The key elements of a mission statement are these: It has to be written down. Not only that but you should write it in the present tense. I *am* a sales professional, not I'd *like to be* a sales professional. The statement should cover a variety of activities and should include vivid descriptions that anchor it to reality. It should be inspiring, exciting, clear, engaging, and it should be specific to you. You have enthusiasm, gifts and unique talents, so it should showcase these. It should cover both your work and your personal life. Get the impression this will take a certain amount of work? Well, remember the words of Plato: "The unexamined life is not worth living."

The only unsuccessful mission statements are low-energy—the ones that do not inspire us because they are bland—or those that are unintelligible to a twelve-year-old. If you use the outline I've provided, you should be able to arrive at a meaningful, vibrant statement for your mission.

Now let's look at goal setting as a separate activity. Once we have a mission statement we need to construct some goals so we have a road map to success. Here's my point of view on goals: if we fail to plan, then we plan to fail. The purpose of goals is to provide a mental target to hit. But not all goals are painted like bull's eyes. We can be enthusiastic about a goal, say like learning computer proficiency. But if we're starting from scratch, we need to gain some skill instruction. Do you know what I mean? Someone to teach me in a mode that says, "I direct you, you do it."

Are any of your goals like that? If so, you need to take a seminar, go to the library or in some other way seek the appropriate training. Then, once you have the competency to establish the goal and run after it, motivation will be the issue. Here again is where the mission statement rescues us. The passion and commitment of the mission statement make motivation so much easier to acquire. And do we ever need that motivation! Some goals offer unexpected roadblocks and potential for disillusionment. Reality is much tougher than expectations.

I once took a course in auto mechanics, figuring it would be fun to learn how to fix up my '66 Mustang. Eighty percent of the class dropped out after two lectures because the course required math homework. The students were disillusioned by the need to learn theory. Their motivation wasn't strong enough to carry them through the hurdle. They wanted to tinker with an engine block, but not for any real purpose. Now, suppose there was a young student in the class room with a mission statement to become a certified auto mechanic. Do you think a little arithmetic homework would stop that person? Of course not. Still other types of goals are really best achieved through a buddy system or a support group, where you have an individual mentor to urge you on. Personal excellence and progress toward challenging goals are not easy to attain. But after developing a mission statement, each of us can embark on the journey—and enjoy the learning, the plateaus and the ride along the way.

Nothing can take the place of determination in goal setting or in life. We need to allow our mission statements to boost our persistence to go on no matter how crushed, defeated or demoralized we may become. If we keep putting one foot in front of the next, according to a purpose, according to a mission, then perseverance and the law of averages will see to it that we succeed with time. Persistence is the essential factor in the procedure of translating goals into reality—persistence and the power of will. Think of these as irresistible forces, indomitable traits. Persistence, strength of will and passionate mission: what an unstoppable combination!

To set goals requires action plans, especially for the most important ones. Once you develop the habit of writing and rewriting your goals, then you can update and improve on them as you go along. The more time you spend on this, the better and more believable the goals become. It's as if the repetition burns them into your subconscious and makes it chase after them—relentlessly, even while you sleep. In fact, reading over your goals just before bedtime activates your subconscious and puts it to work for you overnight. Often ideas will present themselves to you the next day, as if by coincidence. But it isn't a coincidence, it's your subconscious at work, figuring stuff out for you while you sleep.

When listing goals, it is helpful to isolate component parts. Even the biggest goal can be organized into step-by-step pieces. Once you've determined the first step, the second flows logically. Not only that, the goal becomes cooked into your subconscious mind. Setting goals becomes an activity that yields a very high return on the time we invest—perhaps higher than any other activity.

GOAL SETTING WORKSHEET

When properly used, this worksheet will give you information that can enable you to overcome any obstacle toward achieving your goals. A good way to perform the entire exercise is with pen and paper. A better way is to find some privacy and allow yourself at least two hours. The best way *is to treat yourself to a day of solitude during which to think and reflect—quietly and calmly—about your answers to these questions. Do this exercise with candor and diligence; it may very well change your life. This is personally sacred material. Treat it as such and receive boundless rewards from completing the exercise. Ready?* Write everything on a pad of paper.

WARM UP
Get a Glimpse of Your Potential

1. If you could eavesdrop on people talking about you, what would you hope to hear?
2. What does your answer to the previous question prompt you to change about yourself?
3. What are your major excuses for not making this change before now?
4. What are remaining situations in which you blame others for your own lack of success?

NOW YOU'RE BAKING
Rise to the Challenge

1. If you had no fear of failure, what specifically would you do in life?
2. If the opinions or approval of others didn't matter, what would you do differently?
3. What are your own positive qualities that you like?
4. What negative qualities would you rather not have?

SITUATIONS MUST NOT RULE YOU
Taking Responsibility

"Whatever the mind can conceive and believe, it can achieve."—Brian Tracy

You feel positive about yourself to the degree you feel you are in command of your own life. *What parts of your life do you feel are most and least under control?*

You can trace every condition in your life back to a specific cause. *How has cause-and-effect worked in your family, career, health or financial situation?*

Whatever you believe with intense feeling or deeply felt emotion becomes your own reality. Thus, what you expect can become a self-fulfilling prophesy. *Is what you strongly believe in helping you or hurting you?*

You must inevitably attract into your life people and situations that are in harmony with your dominant thoughts. Your outer world is a mirror image of your inner world. *Everything that is in your life today you have attracted to yourself. Are you satisfied with your circumstances and the people around you, or should you make some changes? If so, should you change the people and circumstances, or should you go to work on changing yourself? How?*

YOUR SUBCONSCIOUS MIND
A Gold Vein Ready to Be Tapped

Compile a "dream list" of things you would want to see in your life, if only you could believe they were possible to achieve. Please remember that there are *no limits* to the list. This list is only for you, and no one else, to see.

MODELING
A Skill to Move You Rapidly Toward Goals

1. What three people—living or dead—do you most admire? *Why?*
2. List the qualities of character you admire in others and would like to possess yourself.
3. Rank those qualities you admire in the order of your personal priority.
4. What will you do differently as a result of this information?

SUCCESS

Goal Setting Accelerates It

1. Setting goals has already brought you success to a moderate degree. To demonstrate this, list three goals, large or small, that you have set for yourself and achieved thus far in your life.

2. Now, write your answer to this next question *in no more than one minute:* Currently, what are your three most important goals in life?

3. What would you do, where would you go, and how would you spend your time if you learned today that you have six months to live?

4. What would you do and how would you change your life if you won $5 million in tax-free cash tomorrow?

5. What one great thing would you dare to dream *if you knew you could not fail?*

6. In what areas do you currently have the greatest intensity of purpose?

7. What beliefs are most important to you? Why?

8. What is your individual area of excellence?

9. What will you do differently because of your answers to these questions?

ACHIEVING CLEAR GOALS

1. What is one major, definite goal in your life at the present time?

2. Write down this goal in clear, specific language.

3. Now write down a detailed plan for achieving your goal.

4. What are the possible obstacles standing between you and your goal?

5. Choose one obstacle and describe, step by step, what you can do to overcome it.

6. List possible sources of help and support.

MISSION STATEMENT WORKSHEET

The implications of having a mission statement can be rather daunting at first. You may have to acquire new skills, for example. Some people may even be forced to relocate, because our geographic surroundings must be naturally and positively aligned with our desired achievements. (You can't be a Wisconsin trail guide in Gettysburg, PA). But the penalty for *not* making a mission statement is even more scary, because not to have one leads to confusion and lagging self esteem. Either you are living out your own mission or you are living someone else's. It's your choice.

THE MISSION STATEMENT
What Is It, Anyway?

"A written-down reason for being."—*Steven Covey*

"So simple a twelve-year old should understand it."—*Laurie Beth Jones*

Though you must work toward self knowledge before discerning your mission statement, you will find it is amazingly simple to write it down once you get started. It only takes some people a few hours. When you have a mission, it may broaden over time. That's perfectly okay. The immediate payoff is that you achieve *clarity*—clarity of the type that makes everything easier; from goal setting to time management.

Passion and excitement are the keys. Here's the best way to begin: Think about what most excites you or makes you enthusiastic. Ask yourself what sorts of things do you dwell upon most of the time in these areas: Family . . . Work . . . Health . . . Relationships. List them on a sheet of paper.

Next, *think of three action words* that really hit your hot button . . . words like "teach," "motivate," "solve," or "generate." Think of your own action words and write them down. Then, *think about what principle or activity you would be willing to devote your life to.* For some, this brings to mind a key phrase or value like "joy" or "service" or "family" or "creativity" or "excellence" or "computers." Write down a word or phrase for yourself.

The last piece of this puzzle will be *to think of the group, entity or cause you most would like to help in a positive way.* "Labor relations," "women's issues," "the environment," "fashion," "biotech," "public safety," "health care," "business clients," "the news," or whatever you want to write down.

Once you get this done, go back to your action words (three verbs), add your core values, and for whom it is intended and . . . *Voila!* You will have the basis for your mission statement.

Using the pieces of information you brought to light by performing the exercise on the prior page, write your personal mission statement in the space below.

Write it in the present tense, describing the kind of life that you want to lead based on the positive qualities and values you have identified. Ready?

My mission is to _____, _____, and _____ (your three verbs) _____ (your core value or values) to, for, or with _____ (the group or cause which most excites you).

Does the statement you wrote surprise you? Does it fit you? How do you feel when you say it out loud? A good mission statement will be exciting, inspiring, clear and engaging. It will be specific to you and to your enthusiasms, gifts, and talents. If this isn't the case with your statement, then re-work it until it meets the criteria. Get a thesaurus and find better words. Make it resonate. Keep at this until you can explain the sentence to a twelve-year-old and say it in your sleep.

BONUS
The "WOW" Questions

Here are some provocative questions to help you ponder what it means to become your own person, to discern your true inner nature, and to develop the will to act on your knowledge of self.

1. Where am I now in my life?
2. What meaning does this exercise have in the context of my life as a whole?
3. What is trying to emerge within me at this time? What potential is trying to unfold?
4. Which self images and beliefs of the past must I relinquish to support whatever it is that is emerging from within me?

Taking action without planning is a source of most of life's problems, because it leads to doing things without considering the long-term consequences. The converse is also true: the most successful accomplishments are preceded by a well-designed plan. The better and more complete the plan, the more likelihood for success. The more completely you imagine and visualize the outcome, the greater the chance it will be fulfilled in your life. So always remember to dream and to visualize when setting goals. Don't be afraid of daydreams. Embrace them and put them to work for you.

Forty years ago, Napoleon Hill wrote his classic best seller, *Think and Grow Rich,* and published what was then his startling discovery that we become what we think about most of the time. He studied successful people and found that they did not concentrate on failure. They didn't dwell on mistakes. They didn't worry uselessly about the past. They used their energy to think about their aspirations, their objectives, their dreams and their goals. If you think more often about your own mission, your dreams, your goals—and less about what you don't have— watch what happens.

When you have goals, especially written goals, you begin to lead a purposeful life. Your energy is focused like a laser beam. You become the kind of person who overcomes obstacles. You become harder to distract. Defense Department studies of prisoners of war indicate that those who were the most susceptible to brainwashing were the unfortunate ones whose lives had no defined mission or goal. Those prisoners who possessed centering influences in their personalities were regarded as stubborn resisters. They could see and understand the long-range consequences of giving into the enemy interrogators. The ones with goals and personal missions did not crack. They may have been physically injured from torture and abuse, but their will was indomitable. They triumphed against horrible odds by being unbreakable, by having character and integrity, true grit.

I hope you won't ever undergo torture. But with goals and a mission statement, you will be unlikely to founder on the rocks of some business competition—or the jealously of a professional rival. Keep your goals and purpose in front of your own eyes and watch your progress soar. Of course your goals should have benefits that extend beyond just yourself. Unless your activity is somehow a benefit to others, it is not likely to succeed. For example, happiness can never be a goal because happiness is the logical outcome or byproduct of striving for a purposeful goal. You are not likely to be happier than when you're on the right path, pursuing the goals you have set. It is said that the road to heaven is heaven. Another popular saying is, "It's not the pursuit of happiness, but the happiness of pursuit."

I should mention the important concept of change before leaving this subject. Change is so pervasive that today's average professional person makes more professional decisions in a month than his or her grandparents made in their entire lives.

The three qualities that get you through change are clarity of purpose, which you achieve through setting a mission statement and setting goals; professional competence, which you get by paying your dues, such as attending night school, so that you can develop your own area of excellence for which the economy will reward you; and courage, especially the courage to take responsible risks. Here is the key to getting courage: do the things you fear. Act as if it is impossible to fail. Accept full responsibility for your actions and emotions. Don't blame someone else or something else. Be more open to questioning what you're doing, if you are not getting the results you want.

For people with proper mission statements and goals, *stress* is a helpful barometer rather than a problem. To the degree you have stress when pursuing your mission, something is wrong. You should be able to seek peace of mind, always acting with optimism and perseverance. Not all stress is bad, we now know. Negative stress is best avoided by sticking to your goal plan. You don't waste time and you live true to yourself.

Perseverance is another often-overlooked key to achievement. I took my little boy to a Baltimore Orioles game last summer. While he was eating a hot dog, I began to read the program and realized something about the winning edge for a baseball player, at least for a batter. An Orioles player who gets five hits every twenty at bat has a .250 average and makes five hundred thousand dollars per year. Another Orioles player who gets six hits for every twenty at bat has a .300 average and makes *four million* dollars a year. It may not seem like a lot of difference in performance: one hit in every twenty at bat. But it results in huge difference in compensation.

In business, small differences in results also create dramatic earning differentials. Most of it is due to perseverance as much as anything else. There is a famous rule called the Pareto Principle, which is also called the 80-20 rule. The principle says that 20 percent of your activity always accounts for 80 percent of your earnings. How about this aspect of the rule: 20 percent of the sales force earns 80 percent of the commissions! What you should want is to be in that top 20 percent.

Bookstores are crammed with self-improvement guides, yet the majority of people are underachievers. Procrastination and lack of perseverance are two reasons. Procrastination is for losers. Want to be successful? Study the losers in your profession and avoid doing what they do. You have to believe that for every difficulty that blocks you, there are people who have overcome difficulties ten times as hard and fifty times as fierce.

People blast through obstacles and achieve success when they behave in a manner consistent with their own personal goals. Once you set your goals and get everything to start moving you toward them, you will be acting as intelligently and as successfully as you can all day, every day.

Now let's see where we are in this. I mentioned that your goal should benefit not only you but others. What do others want? They want security, comfort, love and respect. Well, my goodness, let's give it to them. And you can achieve great success in the process. Here are my rules for success as envisioned in your mission statement and goals.

- **Number 1—Dream big!** Set high, challenging goals for your work and personal life. Big dreams give you the energy to take big action. Imagine you could increase your

Self Help

annual current sales commission *ten times.* If you keep repeating the new amount to yourself over and over, it sounds more real. Repeat it enough to believe it, until it becomes your reality.

- **Number 2—Do not dwell upon possible failure, because that will only paralyze you to inaction.** The average self-made millionaire has been broke two or three times. I told you my history on this one.

- **Number 3—Persist until you achieve.** Your ability to persevere will become the single greatest index of your self-esteem. I've learned the hard way that sometimes the only difference between mediocrity and screaming success is an additional five minutes of perseverance.

- **Number 4—Do what you love to do.** If you won a million dollars tax-free tomorrow, what sort of work would you choose to do for the future? Your answer speaks volumes about your personal area of excellence. Until you work in this area of personal excellence you cannot throw yourself into what you do with enough passion to increase your earnings ten times.

- **Number 5—Resolve to learn from your mistakes.** Extract every possible lesson from every experience and become strengthened by it.

- **Number 6—Ask others for help; don't go it alone.** Develop and nurture a support network.

Setting goals and having a mission are things that lead to success. Successful people go beyond the point where the average person would stop, and they are willing to do what the average person will not do. Writing out your mission statement will be an important step to activate forces that will draw that kind of success to yourself.

Don't go to the next chapter before starting work on the form! Good luck and good insights.

In summary . . .

- *Develop a personal mission statement.*
- *Balance and integrate your personal, public, and inner lives.*
- *Follow an action plan to achieve goals.*

If you want to be truly successful invest in yourself to get the knowledge you need to find your unique factor. When you find it and focus on it and persevere your success will blossom.

—*Sidney Madwed*

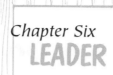

Chapter Six

LEADER

Where Have All the Leaders Gone?

Outstanding leaders appeal to the hearts of their followers—not their minds.

—author unknown

⟹◦⟸

*I*magine that one day you're sitting in elementary school and the teacher asks, "What is your definition of leadership?" What elementary school answer comes into your mind? "Leading other people"? But what would your best response be? Think of a very simple definition. "Having the means to encourage people to follow you"? What else comes to mind? How about "getting people to let you in the front of the line"? Is that all it is—getting people to accept your directions, no matter how valid? Think about leaders of myth and history. The Pied Piper of Hamelin? He got people and rats to follow him! Is that what comes to mind when you hear the word leadership. How about this angle? Maybe a leader is someone who gets you to do what you didn't want to do in the first place.

Confusing, isn't it? The definition I like to use is from a friend of mine. His name is Dudley Davis. His definition of leadership is "the ability to create followship." Not fellowship,

followship. Every time I enter "followship" into my computer, the spell-checker changes it to fellowship. Followship is the word I want. *Leadership is the ability to create followship.* Wouldn't it be neat if the people around you, the people you surround yourself with, followed you? Followed your advice, followed your direction, followed your requests? And not only your clients, but everyone around you?

As I said earlier, you've got to accept people's personality styles and types. But when you become more effective in developing this thing we call followship, you use the ability to become more effective in your church, your synagogue, your civic organizations, your clubs, your work, your home and your family.

As we discuss the essence of leadership, my goal is to have you remember certain beliefs that I hold. Number one is to remember that leaders are not born, they're made. In fact they're self-made. I'll sit down with the CEO of a company who earns a couple of million dollars a year, and we'll be talking about leadership training for the whole sales force. And he'll say

"Steve, come on now, just between you and me, aren't people either born leaders or not born leaders?" And I'll wonder how he made it to such a high compensation level. Leaders are not born, they are always self-made.

Let's look at this notion in more detail. Think about how we are doing in America regarding leadership: are we in the top third, the middle third or the bottom third compared with the rest of the world? I'm afraid I've got bad news for you. We have tragically fewer leaders today in America than we did in the eighteenth century. At the signing of the Declaration of Independence we only had three million people living in America. And yet in Philadelphia, Pennsylvania, not too far from my home, six world-class leaders from different walks of life got together and signed the document. We had Washington, Jefferson, Franklin, Adams, Hamilton, and Madison. Over 220 years later we have 270 million people living in America and you can't name six world-class leaders. Who are you going to start with? Joey Buttafucco? I mean really, who are we going to name? We're hard pressed to identify them, because we have tragically fewer leaders today than we did over 200 years ago.

You know what? Absence of visible leaders is not really our fault. Take a look around and reflect that we are part of the generation that has experienced more change than any other generation in the history of recorded civilization. Thirty years ago my grandfather taught me how to drive a car. This year, my seven-year-old taught me how to reprogram my VCR. The other day my seven-year-old asked my wife, "Mommy, why is Daddy always bringing that briefcase home and going into that little room?" She explained very patiently, "Well, you know, Daddy doesn't have time to get all his work done during the day. So he has to put the remaining work in that briefcase and bring it home at night." And my son looked up and said. "Well, couldn't they just put him on a slower track?"

People living today have experienced more change than anyone else in history. In fact there is a good argument to be made that we are right now living in the middle of a fundamental change due to the information revolution, the Internet, faster and faster download times and the coming of instant access to just about every sort of information. This may very well be a development far more profound than the two previous major changes in civilization, the advancement from hunter-gatherer to productive agriculture five hundred years ago, and the movement from farms to cities in the Industrial Revolution. And now here is this information revolution. It seems impossible to gain perspective on the upheaval while in the middle of it, but we know something profound is going on. So what are we

We gotta take that hill...again?

going to do about it? Accept that there can be no effective leadership method at this time? To use an academic word, "Baloney!"

Let's review a couple of traits of effective leaders. First of all, realize that everyone reading this book has the potential to be a leader. Even an extraordinary leader. You don't have to be tall, you don't even have to be very smart. You can be whatever you are right now and be an incredibly effective leader.

To illustrate good leadership vs. less effective leadership, I'm going to use the example history provides in the persons of some United States Generals. General William Westmoreland was commander of the in-theater forces during much of the Vietnam conflict. General Norman Schwartzkopf was in charge of the fighting forces during Operation Desert Storm for the gulf war. General Colin Powell, who made the transformation from human being to celebrity phenomenon in 1996 during his book signing tour, was formerly chairman of the Joint Chiefs of Staff. Let's look at some differences in these men's leadership performance.

During the Vietnam conflict, General Westmoreland had orders from Washington. His job was not to question them, just carry them out. His performance was evaluated on such things as body count. If you're old enough, you will remember how we'd wake up in the morning and find out on the *Today* show how many enemy forces were obliterated compared to how many American casualties were counted in Vietnam the day before. Vietnam was a troubling conflict: the public seemed not to understand what we were doing there. The soldiers themselves were confused and bothered by the home-front opposition and General Westmoreland's being evaluated daily on such things as relative body count.

If the people in the headquarters tents couldn't question the mission, then the average foot soldier had no clue either. Imagine receiving your orders:

"Take that hill."

"Why?"

"I don't know."

"What happens if we do?"

"I don't know."

"What happens if we don't?"

"I don't know."

It was a war of missed missions, with a significant portion of the public unmercifully critical of the whole effort.

There was a Captain Schwartzkopf in Vietnam at that time. He went on to become the general whom fate placed in charge of the coalition forces during Operation Desert Storm, more than fifteen years after the war in Vietnam. Now here is a difference worth noting: Schwartzkopf said, okay I'll command this effort, but I insist on having all of my staff advisors with me in the room when the strategy is developed. I insist on being part of the strategy and I want all of my advisors to be with me when I hear it. And second, I want you to understand, Joint Chiefs of Staff, that I want every single person who partakes in this conflict, I don't care if they're deployed as potato peelers, to know what the plan is.

So we're talking about two very different scenarios, with two very different outcomes. The social tension that has resulted from the Vietnam era has been described as a generational fault line, a deep rift that will never fully heal until long after everyone involved is no longer on earth, and maybe not even then. The Gulf War ended swiftly in a resounding success in the terms of the military objectives that were sent forth. Afterward, parades and goodwill greeted the returning soldiers.

Now, let's take a look at General Powell. His book, *My American Journey,* was a smash bestseller. His speaking style has been described by Professor Oren Harari of the University of San Francisco, who once shared a platform with him, as "witty, erudite, insightful, articulate and self-deprecating." Powell's book carries gems of wisdom regarding effective leadership. Here is a man who has not only done it, but catalogued it.

Powell has several priceless maxims on leadership in the book. My favorites are:

- **You don't know what you can get away with until you try.** Good leaders don't wait around for official blessings before trying things out. They are not reckless, but they realize that in organizations, if you ask enough people for permission, eventually someone will say, "No." So the moral is, don't ask permission when your gut says go ahead. I'm serious.

- **Organizational charts and fancy titles count for next to nothing.** The capacity to influence or inspire people is the real source of power, and it has little to do with placement on the organizational chart. People with drive, charisma and caring for their teammates will attract more commitment from others regardless of their position on the chart.

- **Great leaders are simplifiers who can offer a solution that everybody can understand.** Using the KISS principle, or Keep it Simple and Straightforward, effective leaders articulate vivid goals and values, and keep their visions lean and compelling. Their decisions are crisp and clear, not tentative and ambiguous. The result? Credibility and integrity for them, and the creation of followship.

- **Have fun—don't always run at a breakneck pace. Surround yourself with people who take their work seriously, who work hard, but also play hard.** Seek to associate with people who have some balance in their lives and who are fun to hang around with and who have some non-job priorities about which they are as passionate as their work. Avoid the grim workaholics.

The main lesson to take from all of this is that you and I need certain rules to go by when we're trying to be effective leaders. The people you surround yourself with include your children, your significant other, your neighbors, your co-workers, your clients and customers. All of them have certain rights, something like a bill of rights.

The first right they have is to be part of the strategy, to be involved in the strategy, to know what the heck the strategy is. The second right they have is the right to influence their own destiny. "What if we take the hill? What will happen?" They must know how taking that hill affects their own destiny. So explain the consequences if they do not follow your leadership.

A book called *Flight of the Buffalo* talks about leadership as well as bison. In a herd of buffalo, say two hundred head, how many of the animals know where they are going? One! If that lead buffalo takes a wrong turn and goes over a cliff, 199 other buffalo will hurtle over the cliff after him. You say, that's animals. But is it? In a flock of geese, how many geese know where they are going? All of them! They all know they're going to Ft. Lauderdale for the winter. Right? So when two or three of them break out of the pattern and die or disappear, the rest of them reconfigure and keep on going. I urge you let everyone know what your strategy is and thereby surround yourself with geese instead of buffalo.

I started to implement some of these procedures with my own children. I have three boys, two little guys and a teenager. Because of my travel schedule I'm gone most weekdays. When I come home Friday night after being in five different cities, my wife says "I love you, but here are the boys." And utter chaos breaks out. My seven-year-old wants to play ball, my eight-year-old wants to go to the library, my teenager wants to go to the movies. So I take a chapter out of my own book. We sit down on Saturday mornings and come up with a strategy. I involve them in the strategy. And you wouldn't believe the balance of the weekend. They follow me around like little ducks. First, we'll go to the movies. Then we'll go to the ball game. They all cooperate because they are all involved in developing the strategy. There is nothing more powerful than letting people know what they can do for themselves.

A fundamental thing for a leader to do is define reality. When I sit down with my kids on Saturday morning, I let them know that traveling on the Concorde to London is not one of the options this weekend. The first thing you must do for others is

Follow Me e e e e e . . .

define the limits of reality. Another important thing a leader should do is to say *thank you*. It's not difficult, you know. This is not quantum physics after all, just basic common-sense human relations. Define reality, and say thank you.

Was Lee Iacocca a good leader? Sure he was. Was he a good manager? I'm afraid not. He got fired, demoted, fired, demoted, voted out and sued, so he wasn't necessarily successful as a manager. But he was one heck of a leader. Lee Iacocca, when he presided over Chrysler, walked on to the assembly line one day when a car was coming off the line. At that time, the Big Three car manufacturers had been out of the convertible business for years because of safety issues. We just weren't making convertibles in the United States. Iacocca walked up to the line where a little hard-top car was coming off and made small talk with the engineer. The engineer gulped, my goodness, here is the big boss chit-chatting. Then Iacocca asked the question he'd come to ask: "How long would it take to make this model into a convertible?" The engineer thought for a moment and said, "Well, to do it right we'd have to send it over to Safety, then to Design, route it by Modeling, then schedule it for production. This could be a convertible probably in twelve to fourteen months. Lee said, "Well, I want to drive it home tonight as a convertible. I'll meet you here at five," and walked away. Just like that.

"The Convertible"

The engineer went to the bathroom, came back and hurriedly gathered a team of people with blow torches. They ripped the top off, covered the gash with masking tape and spray painted the chassis. Lee walked in at 5:05 and drove home in a convertible. On the ride, he wore glasses and a hat so no one knew who he was. But all he could hear and see were beeping horns and hands waving and thumbs-up signs. The next day Chrysler Corporation went into the convertible business. How did they do? Whoa! Massively well. Did any of the car makers follow them into the convertible business? Everyone did! The return to convertibles was a huge success!

This anecdote helps illustrate a key difference between managers and leaders. Managers do things right. Leaders do the right thing. So every once in a while you need to pull yourself off whatever treadmill you are riding and ask, "I know I'm doing things right, but am I doing the right things?"

In summary, leaders aren't necessarily born, they're made and almost always self-made. The first thing a leader should do is define reality. You should surround yourself with people and allow them to be part of the strategy. You should allow people you surround yourself with to affect their own destiny. At the end of the day, say thank you to anyone who has contributed to the success of your endeavors. That's pretty simple, and if you do it, you will create followship, from members of your family, right through to your company and customers.

In summary . . .

- *Create followship.*
- *Make yourself a leader.*

I learned that a great leader is a man who has the ability to get other people to do what they don't want to do and like it.

—*Harry Truman*

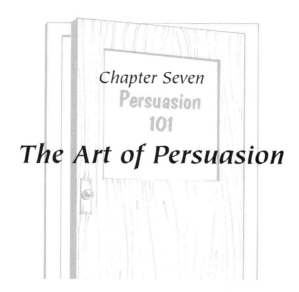

Chapter Seven
Persuasion
101

The Art of Persuasion

Remember that a person's name is to that person the sweetest and most important sound in any language.

—Dale Carnegie

———◆———

We now have a little consultative selling and a little leadership under our belts. You've created relationships, you've created followship, and you have a personal mission. Now I want you to get down to the blocking and tackling of persuasion. I want to get right down to the details of how we make it work. How do I write this contract? How many of my products is the customer going to buy? So let's talk a little bit about influence, because once you have cultivated a customer relationship, you have to actually affect the contract.

You and I have to decide the how much, the when, and the where of the order. So here's an area where a little skill pays off, as well as the ability to influence others to do things your way. Now if I can help you to get your way more often, will that be good for you? Sure! I want you to be able to sell more effectively, to be a more effective resource person. I want you to be able to create followship and become a more effective leader. But I also want you to be able to get your way more often. Wouldn't that be fun? Here are a few tips, *a la* Father Guido Sarducci, that are going to help you get your way more often.

Do you remember Father Guido? He was a comic figure on *Saturday Night Live,* where a comedian played him as an Italian priest. I know a lot about Italians. My aunt's names are Bina, Rena, Gena, Pena, Tina and Maria, no lie. So Father Guido Sarducci said that he was going to start a "Seven-a-Minute-a University." He was going to teach in just seven minutes what a college graduate remembers five years after graduation. While the skit was facetious, I always thought he had a great point, because here I am trying to teach you about consultative selling, leadership, productivity and influence in a book that can be read in a few hours. But Guido had a good skit. He'd say "Okay, we're going to start the seven-a minute university right now. We got to have a science, someone pick a science." And someone in the audience would yell "Physics."

He'd say, "Physics, physics, okay. We only got about nine seconds for physics class, so I can only teach you one thing. *What goes up must come down.* Now you go away to college and take physics 101, 102, 201, 202, and five years later what do you remember about physics? What goes up must come down. Now, we also should have a business. Because everyone's going to grow up, get a job and buy a car. And we should have a business course. Who wants a business course?" The audience would yell "economics."

"Economics!" he'd screech. "Okay we only gotta fourteen seconds for economics class. So we can only learn one thing: *Buy low, sell high.* You'd be surprised at how many people screw thatta one up." And he went on and did a little bit from each subject like that. Boy, that routine used to crack me up.

Well, that's what I'm going to do about persuasion now— just give you the highlights. Because you know what? Carnegie Mellon University published research showing that when

you study summarized material, you achieve a higher level of comprehension, and one year later you remember more of the material, too. So we're not going to go into all of persuasion. There are a hundred books on persuasion and fifty more on negotiation that we can avoid by doing it this way.

We have a global economy now. Let's begin by asking ourselves how we are doing in the area of business influence as Americans. You guessed it! Horribly! The only reason we've gotten our way is because we have more money than anyone else, more resources. How much money did the company lose last quarter? It was 1.1 million dollars. That's too bad, maybe we'll do better next quarter. Let's go to lunch. After that we'll throw some more resources at the problem. Assign a few more vice presidents to the project, that'll do it.

Until recently, all we've had to come up with are more corporate resources, and they seemed unlimited. Welcome to the new millennium! I don't care if you're with Intel, Xerox, or Orange County, California. We no longer have endless resources of money, time, people and things. So we've got to get better at influencing other people to strike a more favorable deal with us.

The number one thing you and I should do differently when we want to sell something is to stop requesting the "fair" price. The concept of "fairness" before the fact, that is, a predetermined idea of what each side "should" accept, really hampers your results. Oh, you should have a goal in mind. Just don't open your discussion by tossing your goal on the table and saying, "This is fair." In some parts of the world it baffles the locals how something could be "fair" before any haggling takes place. Since America is a melting pot of world influences, you cannot assume that your counterpart will buy into your unique notion of what is "fair" before you two have attempted to trade back and forth a bit.

Stop opening at your desired goal. Say you have an automobile you want to sell. It's in your garage. It's worth about ten thousand dollars. You'd be happy to get ten thousand dollars for it. In fact, you checked with your spouse, who saw two of them across town at ten thousand dollars a piece. Your neighbor works for the National Auto Dealers Association and he checked the blue book and told you that's a very good price. You call your banker and say "I want to sell that thing in my garage." She says, "That will be fine, but you've got to pay off the ten thousand dollars loan." So let's think about it. You have to get ten thousand dollars for the car; you'd be happy with ten thousand dollars, because it is a fair price.

So you put an ad in the local newspaper, offering to sell your car for ten thousand dollars. Someone calls you up and offers eight thousand. What do you have to say? "No, I need ten thousand dollars and these are the reasons why. My wife, my banker, blah, blah, blah." And if you're lucky, the next thing they'll say is how about nine thousand? Once again, you have to say, "No, I need ten thousand dollars. Did I tell you the reasons why? Blah, blah, blah." If you're real lucky the caller will offer ninety-five hundred. Once again, you tell him, "No, I need ten thousand dollars and these are the reasons why, in case you didn't hear me the first two times." What happens next? Click, he hangs up. Click, negotiations break down between owners and the players. *Click,* negotiations break down between the two countries. *Click,* negotiations break down between Caterpillar and the union. It happens all the time.

Poor negotiators figure out in advance what they want and they ask for it. Good negotiators figure out what they want and they ask for *more.* Why do they ask for more? Because they're greedy? No they ask for more so they can give away some ground!

Before you enter into another business interaction, where you want to persuade someone to do something your way, first take the time to decide what the heck it is you should want. Many times people do not fare too well in a negotiation because they do not bother to figure out beforehand what it is they want. You may have fallen into this trap. It's common; I've done it many times. So before you enter into your next interaction, I want you to figure out what you want. When you know what you want, call that desired position your **target outcome.** It can be a target date, a target quantity, a target time, whatever. But it's the outcome you prefer, if the discussions go reasonably well.

Next, before you begin talking, use your intelligence, your experience, your knowledge, and your due diligence to come up with a **more aggressive position.** Come up with a stiff request that is not what you would expect to receive, but which is at least arguably reasonable, and *begin there.* Why do we start an interaction such as this with a more aggressive position? For one reason, and one reason only: so that we can give it up and make the other party feel good about wresting concessions from us. When the other side can show something, they will feel as if they've done well—which they will have.

So before you enter into an interaction like this, I want you to figure out what the heck it is you want. Call that your target. Then I want you to come up with a bit more aggressive position and start the interaction there. You do that for one reason, and one reason only: so that you can give. And the third thing I'd like you to do is to figure out ahead of time how low you can go, how far you can extend, how much of an exception you can make before this deal no longer makes any sense. Call that your **bottom line.** If you do that your life will change as a persuader.

I guarantee you that in every one of these interactions, the other side is going to ask you for something. Can I start later? Can you finish it earlier? Can I pay less? Can you give me more? They're going to ask you for something, without fail. So ask yourself, when you ask someone to give in during a sales negotiation, what do you want to hear? You want to hear the word "yes." Think about what happens when you muster the courage to ask someone for a concession, hoping to hear "yes," and the answer is "no." What happens to the climate? It becomes cold, antagonistic; a chill descends. I mean it's not very favorable. So, let me see, when I ask people for something and I want them to say yes, maybe that means when people ask *me* for something, maybe *they* want *me* to say yes! If you start with a higher position, you have room to say yes.

Am I suggesting that you should say yes to every request? No, your company would go out of business with each deal, one by one. All I'm saying is that you have another alternative. Here's an example. I stayed overnight in a Hyatt Regency at Chicago O'Hare about two years ago, and I paid $220 for the room. In the morning I went down to the front desk and asked whether I could please have another key to my room. The very pleasant desk person looked at me and said, "No." She may as well have jumped across the desk and punched me in the face. "Thank you for staying with us and spending your 220 bucks, but NO." Now, why did she say no? Frankly, she had a reason to say no, because it was 8 a.m. and I had already lost two keys to my room. So the third time she felt justified in saying no. But I made a suggestion to her in a very pleasant way. I suggested that instead of saying, "No, you can't have another key," she could have said, "Yes, Mr. Wiley, we can give you another key to your room, *if* you allow the bellman to follow you up to the room, and you give him the two keys you already lost this morning, you idiot you." The only thing I would have

No Key

heard was "YES." Well maybe I would have heard "you idiot," too, but I swear it wouldn't have bothered me.

Other people simply don't like to hear you say no. If someone asks you for a favor, instead of saying no, try to think creatively. Think of a way to say, **"Yes if."** Yes, we could drop the price 10 percent *if* you buy two of them. Yes, we could do that *if* you waited until next quarter to take delivery. Yes, we could do that *if* you take the blue ones. Yes, we could do that *if* we remove color altogether. "Yes, *if*" is light years ahead of saying *no*. Does it work all the time? No, it doesn't work all the time. But, my goodness, it will work most of the time.

You can even use it to lighten the mood, to add some humor to a potentially aggravating situation. A friend of mine is in charge of advertising at a newspaper, a customer called him and said, "Scott, I love your paper and I want to advertise next month. Last month you gave me a 15 percent discount. Is it possible I have an 84 percent discount this month?" And Scott was thinking, "Oh, jeez. I took that class from Steve Wiley and I'm supposed to say 'Yes, *if*.' So he stammered, "Yes, if, er, yes, if I were *stupid* I could do that."

You can't say yes to everything and anything. Supply and demand will always overrule these tips. But "yes, *if*" will get you a long, long way.

Another tip is to make several small concessions throughout the negotiation itself. You start high so that you can give things away. But make small concessions. I've asked you to please figure out what you want and call it your target. Come up with a bit more aggressive position for you and your company, start there and call it your opening. You need to create room for give and take, and, I hope, end up where you want to be in terms of your target position. In case you cannot achieve that—and there are many times when it is not possible to get everything you want, let's face it—you will have already figured out your bottom line. Knowing this will help you stay aware of how much you can give up and still accept a deal.

Now, do you start high in order to have an argument? No, you start high so you can give ground. People in our "fair-minded" society have trouble with this, more than you would think. If you can persuade yourself to start high, you're half way home, even before the discussion takes place.

People often make this mistake: They would be happy with ten grand for the car. They think, "That guy Steve says I should ask for more. I don't feel good about that, I feel like I need to take a shower after this, but I'll do it. I've done some research and twelve thousand dollars would be reasonable for a pristine car of that model and year. Pristine is something my car is not. But okay, I'm asking twelve thousand."

They start high, but the other party says, "Can't you do any better than that?"

They say, "Sure, I'll take ten thousand," and they are right back at the "fair" position, and now they have to say no if the other side asks for more concessions. Keep making concessions, just make them small, so you can make them more often.

Always be aware of your ego throughout this process. Be aware of your own false ideas about competition. Be aware of your instinct to win, because those instincts, John Wayne and all the sports programs you ever watched or played, teach you that the other side must lose in order for you to win. This stuff requires patience to be done right. And you're thinking, "I don't have time to be patient." Is that true, or is it that patience never gets priority in our busy world?

There seem to be more books on time management than anything in the world. Because you are reading a book of this nature, it is likely that you have taken a Franklin Planner session or another course in time management. You are probably aware there are different schools of thought: one says we should eliminate all time wasters and concentrate only on productive tasks. Another says that until we set goals we can't even define productive tasks. And yet another says that productive tasks are an illusion of the mind. What are you supposed to do with all this conflicting direction?

Well, what I've done is distilled all this information using the method of my friend Father Guido Sarducci. What I found is that in every method, you complete a to-do list. The funny thing about to-do lists is that you're supposed to write them out and check things off as you do them. I have a question for you: what happens if you do something that isn't shown on the list? I'll tell you what happens: you go back, put it on the list and check it off. It seems pretty silly to me.

But here are some tips, three little tips to help you with your time management. First, make the to-do list and always indi-

Simplify

cate some kind of priority for the items on the list. Let's say you have items 1 through 20. Well, put 1 through 20 but list them in order of importance. And don't leave number 2 until you're done with number 2. Don't go from number 2 to number 9 to number 6. If the items are prioritized in order of importance and you do 2, 20, 18, 6, 5, you contradict the purpose of your own list.

In terms of your effectiveness as a resource professional, a wonderful thing to discover is what your customers' to-do lists contain, and what their priorities are.

Second, your to-do list is worthless if you don't show any objectives. So along with your to-do list, which is just today's treadmill activity, write down your objectives. Show your objectives in black and white on paper and don't let those objectives disappear from the list until they have been accomplished.

The third thing is to simplify your work space. The only things on your desk should be your to-do list, your objectives, and the task you are working on right now. How's that for simple? Maybe now you can be more patient with clients and customers.

To sum up the art of persuasion, figure out what you want before you enter into an interaction. Start with a more aggressive position so that you can give ground, and therefore the other side can feel that they are doing well. And always know your bottom line before the interaction begins. Say "yes, *if*" instead of no. Say "yes, *if*" instead of yes. And make concessions, but make sure they're small concessions.

And in order to find enough time to be patient, use some basic time management strategies. Keep a to-do list, and keep it prioritized. Have a list of objectives to go along with it, and every day work on three things: your to-do list, your objectives and the task on your desk.

In summary . . .

- *Yes, if . . .*
- *Ask for more to give more away.*
- *Small concessions count for a lot.*
- *Be patient.*

Chapter Eight

Dead Sales Professionals Rarely Make Quota

Happiness lies, first of all, in health.
—*George William Curtis*

⇒◈⇐

*T*his whole area of personal productivity assumes something, doesn't it? It takes for granted we'll be feeling well, both mentally and physically. People who are crabby, tired, unfocused, sick, moody or irritable are not productive. I don't care who we are, we're just not productive. Now rest easy as you read this: I'm not just one more person who's going to tell you to eat fruits and vegetables and exercise more. We all know that right?

I have a great friend from college who experimented with every recreational pharmaceutical there was. The guy was a drug addict, plain and simple. Ten years after college we ran into each other and I said, "How are you doing?" He said, "I tell you I've been through hell. I've lost a couple of wives, a few houses, several cars, a dozen jobs, and spent forty thousand dollars on drug rehabilitation. Then Ronald Reagan gets elected; his wife, Nancy, goes on this war against drugs; and I find out after all that, I could have just said no!"

99

Ahh... But have I mentioned the features and benefits?

There's a lot more to it, isn't there? My friend knew he shouldn't be taking drugs. But it wasn't going to help him to have someone telling him not to do it. Likewise you and I don't need someone to tell us we should eat more fruits and vegetables. We all know we should do that. We all know it's better than eating a lot of sugar and high fat. What we need is someone to tell us *how* to do that.

What made the most profound impact on my adult life, regarding my health, was my experiences at the Pritikin Longevity Centers located in Miami Beach, Florida and Santa Monica, California. My good friends Joan Mikas, Paul Lehr, Kevin Wiser, and Robert Pritikin not only changed my life but the lives of over 70,000 people. I urge you to give them a call to receive further information. Their numbers are 1-800-327-4914 and 1-800-421-9911 respectively.

It takes about twenty years for the effects of a lifestyle (and this includes diet) to catch up with you. After that, it begins to take its toll. People have heart bypass operations, chemotherapy and all sorts of sad medical interventions. And yet we all know we shouldn't eat certain things, don't we?

Let me borrow your imagination for a minute, and an excerpt from Nathan Pritikin's book. Visualize a society in which everyone loved arsenic. They sprinkled it into their coffee, they stirred it into their soup, they baked it into their bread, they grilled their meat with it. It was the most sought-after food enhancer. They couldn't imagine preparing a food without it. But people were starting to get sick. They got stomach aches, they got headaches. Their hair fell out, their teeth fell out. They started to drop dead at the lunch table. They started to drop dead on the golf course. And the rumor went around that maybe it was due to the arsenic. So the pharmaceutical companies started to combat it by coming out with pills for headache, pills for stomachache. The dental profession came out with better false teeth. The hair restoration society came out with better wigs. But people kept getting sick, and they kept dropping dead.

There was one man who was really sick, sicker than most patients. He was forty years old. The doctor said, "You know, you're not going to make it; you won't live more than a week or two. You'd better have your children come in and say good-bye." Now this patient was a bright man, and he was a researcher. He had been conducting research into other societies in this world that didn't eat arsenic. He discovered that people there got sick far less often. So he decided then and there to stop eat-

ing arsenic, and he turned down the tray of food brought to him by the hospital, requesting arsenic-free meals after that.

The results were not only remarkable, they were miraculous. So he started publishing papers, reporting, "I stopped eating arsenic and I got better." And the next thing you know, the dairy association came out with 98 percent arsenic free milk. Cookie companies came out with one-third less arsenic in their cookies. But people kept getting sick.

Now this is not an episode from the *Twilight Zone*. And we're not talking about arsenic. We're talking about our own society, and we're talking about fat, cholesterol and salt. And the sick person in the story was Nathan Pritikin, the person who founded the Pritikin Longevity Center. And his son Robert, a good friend of mine, continues his work. Nathan Pritikin was the first person to link cholesterol and fat to heart disease. This was in 1976. In 1985, *60 Minutes* did a big story on him, and everybody found out about his work.

Today, you can't listen to the radio or read a newspaper without someone talking about eating less fat or exercising more or how fat is not good for you. We are bombarded with bits of information throwing guilt at us for adopting a Western diet of affluence that is killing us. How about this factoid? The first sugar refineries in Europe were built in Napoleon's time. It was he who had them built. Up until then, at the beginning of the nineteenth century, a mere two hundred years ago, the average European consumed seven pounds of sugar each year, and it was expensive and difficult to obtain. Then, the Industrial Revolution and better transportation brought affordable sugar to nearly everyone. The result? Today, the average American consumes 120 pounds of sugar a year, *about seventeen times as much* as the people in Napoleon's time.

Our concern about the damage we are doing via the knife and fork has given birth to a whole new industry. We've got Jenny Craig, we've got Weight Watchers, we've got the grapefruit diet, we've got the chocolate diet. We've got grown men crying on television and bald ladies screaming at us. We have never had more of an emphasis on diet in the history of our world. How are we doing? Are we doing okay? I'm afraid not. We're fatter and sicker than we've ever been. You might be thinking, "This book is delivering some pretty bad news. We don't sell very well, we're not very effective as leaders, and now we're fatter and sicker than we've ever been." Well, friendly reader, once again it's not our fault. It's not our fault. We've just assumed that that's the way life goes. We get older, we get sicker, we get fatter and we die.

You may have watched Billy Crystal in *City Slickers*. It was a great movie. In it, he went to his son's fourth grade class to give a talk as a parent. He spoke to them about what it's like to age. And this is our attitude about aging, unfortunately. He said, "Enjoy this time in your life, children, because you'll spend your twenties wondering where your teens went. You'll spend your thirties wondering where your twenties went. In your forties you'll grow a pot belly, lose some hair and the music will start getting louder. In your fifties you'll have an operation (you'll call it a procedure, but it's an operation). The music will keep getting louder, but you won't mind because you can't hear it as well. In your sixties you'll retire to Ft. Lauderdale, start eating dinner at three in the afternoon, lunch at ten in the morning, and breakfast the night before. And in your seventies you'll start walking around malls eating frozen yogurt and saying, "Why don't the grandchildren call?" In your eighties you'll fall in love with a Jamaican nurse whom your wife hates but you call 'Mama.' Any questions?"

Billy Crystal spoke to our perception of how we get older, we get sicker, we get weaker, we get less productive, then we die. And it doesn't have to be. We wonder why we feed our bodies the wrong food—precisely the wrong food. A diet is 180 degrees off what we should be eating. We have to stop and realize that Madison Avenue has its hand in this. Television is on for so many hours a day that it is estimated that we now watch an average of 900,000 commercials in our lifetime.

Unfortunately two-thirds of those commercials will tell us to eat more or drink more of the wrong thing. And the problem I have with these commercials is that they always depict people as having a good time. Think about it. You're sitting on your couch at home. You're overweight, you're crabby and you're drinking a soda—and there's a commercial on TV advertising the same drink. But the actors have bikinis on. They're good looking women, good looking men; they're sky diving, they're roller blading, they're having a wonderful time. So you look at your soda, you look at your TV, you look back at your soda and you think, "Hey, maybe I'm not using enough ice."

Let's face it, television is a culprit. Here is a piece of data from the Census Bureau: 97 percent of the households in America have a television set, and only 94 percent have indoor plumbing. Great, eh? One of the problems we have is that we've got a perfect way to get all of this crap into the house, but not a very effective way to get it back out! So we adopt lifestyle choices even though twenty years later they give us high blood pressure, adult onset diabetes, obesity, heart disease and several forms of cancer. You don't think advertising is powerful? In 1994 the National Cancer Institute spent four hundred thousand dollars trying to get people to eat more fruits and vegetables. In that same year a leading cereal manufacturer spent sixty *million* dollars advertising a cereal that had the highest sugar and fat content on the market. We wonder why we're having a problem? My goodness.

Can you imagine being in the marketing division of one of those companies, advertising food that's bad for people? I've got a slogan for them. How about a soup that's full of salt and fat. How about this for a slogan: "Mmm-mmm dead." Another one I think is just great would be for some kind of a cookie that has enough fat for you to exceed the recommended weekly allowance: "Give us a week, we'll stop your heart!" I really cannot imagine being involved in advertising cigarettes. If it were up to me, the label on the package might say, "Hey buddy, low birth weight is going to be the least of your problems." I guess I wouldn't make very much money advertising some of these goods.

At the same time, we can't blame it all on Madison Avenue. We have created the ultimate irony on nature. The very reactions that developed to protect us from nutritional deficiency are now killing us from the diseases resulting from our new-found abundance. I would like to see if I can help you out of this trap.

The fact is, ladies and gentlemen, I lost fifty pounds in 1989 and I've kept it off. I was on blood pressure medication for years. Since 1989, I have not taken one beta blocker, not one blood pressure pill, and recently my blood pressure was 120 over 80. How did I do it? Because of my discipline! No, actually, I love to eat, I love Miller Light Beer, I love ice cream, I love Mexican food, I love life. Then how did I do it? Once again, with the help of the Pritikin Longevity Centers, I found out that this thing we call our body is a very sophisticated bio-chemical machine that was adapted to ensure the survival of our cavemen ancestors hundreds of thousands of years ago. And guess what? There is no owner's manual for this machine. I have a can opener with a three-page owner's manual, and yet for the most sophisticated machine on earth, I don't have an owner's manual.

Hundreds of thousands of years ago, men and women fueled this machine ten, eleven, or twelve times a day. Today 58 percent of our calories come in one meal. Maybe that wouldn't be in the owner's manual. A hundred thousand years ago 89 percent of our intake was fruit and vegetables. Today over 90 percent of our intake is fat and chemicals. Maybe that wouldn't be in the manual. A hundred thousand years ago, we were pretty active. We were digging up potatoes, picking fruit, and running away from mountain lions. Today three-fourths of Americans don't exercise at all. The only reason I'm here, and you're here reading this book, is because our ancestors survived periods of famine. Your prehistoric ancestors and my ancestors were able to crawl into a cave and go for long periods without fresh food. Now how did they do it? They did it because this unbelievable machine had developed something for them called the "fat instinct." Today we talk about survival of the fittest. Well in neolithic times, it was survival of the fattest.

When winter came, prehistoric people couldn't find fresh food because everything was frozen. They couldn't dig up potatoes, couldn't pick fruit. The calorie reduction signaled to their body that winter was coming. The fat instinct said, "Go get some fat and hang on to it." The biological machine called the body reduced their metabolism so they would be able to store fat. Not only that, the ingestion of fat triggered a further craving for fat, which in the modern animal kingdom (and in human oases such as the Outback Steakhouse) created a reflex known as *gorging*. This means that eating fat makes you crave more fat. In caveman times, this craving for fat had the effect of keeping people alive throughout the winter, when meals would be severely reduced and days without food of any type were not uncommon. In that environment, carrying a little extra fat made good sense.

So what does this evolutionary background mean for me today? Well, we still have that caveman body. When we take in fewer calories, we trigger the fat instinct. Have you ever tried to lose weight by cutting down on calories? I know I have. As soon as you cut down on calories you signal your body that winter is coming, which is like saying to it on a biological level, "Hang onto the fat and go get some more if you can."

To combat this effect, my tip for you is to *eat more often*. Don't allow the fat instinct to be triggered due to your bodily

Summer   Winter

sensation of food emptiness. Eat more often so your body doesn't think it's going to starve. After all, is starvation a problem these days? Not really. We've got a few inventions to help us out, like the refrigerator.

So here you are, trying to lose weight, trying to be disciplined about it. Mother Nature says get some fat. You resist, saying "No, Mother, my discipline will see me through." Who's going to win that battle? Mother Nature, every single time. So my first tip for you is eat more often, because if you let yourself get hungry between breakfast and lunch you're going to crave the wrong things. This has nothing to do with willpower. It has nothing to do with whether you're a good person or not. It has nothing to do with discipline. It has everything to do with our biological machine, which is afraid of starving. Amid the abundance of food in our culture, there are grossly overweight people in America who spend most of their time going from meal to meal, trapped in ballooning bodies that, ironically, fear they are starving!

In prehistoric times, our bodies were very active. Our ancestors were always walking and running around during the day. Then winter came and they cuddled up into a cave, reduced bodily activity and triggered the fat instinct. The body thought, "Uh-oh, winter's here, better slow down the metabolic rate." Princeton University has studies that show that when we do not exercise, our metabolic rate decreases by 33 percent. What a fix that puts us in! We get fatter, our metabolism declines, yet our bodies want more fatty food. Twenty-five years of this and we are on the operating table.

So, the remedy is to take a walk. Don't go out and try to run a marathon right away. People who haven't exercised in fifteen years make a New Year's resolution and say, "OK, I'll go out tomorrow and I'm going to start an exercise program. I think I'll jog to L.A. and back." And they sprain an ankle and don't exercise for six more weeks. Neither do you have to join a gym and start power lifting. Just go take a walk.

Simply by taking a walk every day, you're signaling your body that springtime is here. Hey Metabolism, everything is coming up roses. *Burn baby burn.* Then you won't crave fat as much. When you want to eat, pick up a tomato.

⟫◆⟪

The sovereign invigorator of the body is exercise, and of all the exercises walking is the best.

—*Thomas Jefferson*

⟫◆⟪

In summary, if you eat more often, your body won't be afraid of starving. You won't need as many calories. If you take a walk, your body will think it's springtime and your metabolic rate will increase. It's that simple!

Here is another health tip for you. What's the third leading cause of absenteeism in America today? Not going to work? Yeah, that will do it every time! But really, it's lower-back pain. Lower-back pain is the leading cause of absenteeism in America today. Thirty eight billion dollars of lost time in America today because of lower back pain. What's the leading cause of lower-back pain? Weakening stomach muscles—stomach flabbiness and loss of muscle mass with advancing years.

This flabbiness doesn't have to plague us. Cornell University finished a study where people in their seventies, eighties and nineties tripled the strength in their stomach through six weeks of doing situps. Okay? Do situps or do stomach crunches, which is a variant that puts less stress on your neck during the exercise. Let me tell you about the first sit-up I did after not exercising for ten years. I barely got my head off the ground. But after about a week I could do a few of them comfortably. After a couple of weeks, I could do several.

You see, getting older means not having the strength and the agility we used to have. That's all it is, and you can triple your strength into your nineties. So do a couple of daily situps in your thirties, forties and fifties. It will mean a lot to you. You can lose weight, look and feel better, be more energetic, and avoid lower-back pain.

It's the afternoon and you are on the phone making outgoing marketing calls. What's on your mind? Food! Are you at your best? Heck no! You protest, "Steve, I'm a professional." I don't care. First of all you're an animal, and animals have cravings. You say, "I have discipline to overcome my cravings." Baloney.

So please make it a regular point to eat breakfast. Then eat small healthy meals often throughout the day. Take a walk and do some situps. I do these things daily and I feel marvelous.

In summary . . .

- *Eat more often, do some sit-ups, and go for a walk everyday.*
- *A healthy lifestyle makes a healthy life.*

Some people lose their health getting wealthy and then lose their wealth gaining health.
—author unknown

Chapter Nine

The Barber Who Knew It All

*I*n urging you to adopt the tips I've presented in this book, I want to emphasize that I have the utmost respect for what you do, especially to the degree it involves selling. Selling is in my bones, and for all my adult life. I have done it for a living. I just hope I haven't come across as a know-it-all. Nobody likes a know-it-all, whether a speaker, an author, a mother-in-law, a policeman, or a barber or hairdresser.

Do you have a barber or a hairdresser that is a know-it-all? I had a friend, Charlie, who hated his barber because he was such a darn know-it-all. His wife said, "You've got to get your hair cut; we're about to go on a vacation we've been planning for a year." They were going to Europe. He said, "I don't want to do that, I hate the barber." But she made him go.

He sat down in the chair and his barber said, "Hey Charlie, what are you doing this summer?"

Charlie said, "I'm going to go on vacation."

"You don't want to go on vacation," said the barber. "Summertime is a bad time. Where are you going?"

"I'm going to Europe."

"Oh, what a silly thing to do, it's expensive. Where are you going in Europe?"

"I'm going to Italy."

"Italy, ahh, it's going to be hot and crowded. What are you going to do in Italy?"

"Well, I'm going to try to see the Pope."

"Ha, ha, see the Pope, yeah, right. He will look like a tiny ant on the balcony. There'll be ten thousand pushy Italians around you. Have a good time!"

Charlie said, "I hate that barber."

Blah Blah Blah

"The Barber"

He went on vacation and he came back. He needed another haircut. He walked into the barbershop and the barber said, "Did you go on vacation yet? Was it expensive like I told you?"

"Yeah."

"Was Italy hot and crowded like I told you it would be?"

"Yeah, it was."

"Did you go see the Pope? Was it just like I told you?"

"Yeah," said Charlie suddenly. "Except when the Pope talked to me."

The barber said, "The Pope talked to you?"

"Yup, it was just like you predicted. He was just a tiny ant on the balcony. But then he came down on the piazza and walked through ten thousand people, and came right up to me."

The barber couldn't believe his ears. "What did the Pope say to you?" he demanded.

"He came up and he grabbed me by the back of the head and said, "Who the devil cuts your hair?"

All of us who have done a lot of selling have a funny story about our most interesting sales call. Mine happened about fifteen years ago. We were in the business of doing oil changes on premise. We would go to Federal Express and ask if we could change the oil in their vehicles during the night so they could use the trucks all day. With our night-time service, customers didn't have to take their trucks to Jiffy Lube. We came to them. So my most terrific salesperson, Terry Smith, and I went to Fort Meade, Maryland, to pitch the base on servicing all its vehicles. There was a new colonel there, and he was fooling with a phone he had just installed, one with a speaker box, which was a new gadget back then.

We waited outside until we heard him say, "Send those guys in." So we entered the office and met him. He was a big man, really huge. We were nervous, we sat down, and we did features and benefits, features and benefits, features and benefits.

And he said, "Okay, I'll give you a trial. You can service one of the motor pools and if it works well, we'll let you do more of them."

He leaned over and pressed the speaker box and we heard, "Motor Pool."

"Yeah, how many vehicles do we have down there in section 9?"

The voice on the intercom said, "Uh, 14 half tracks, 6 jeeps and a Cadillac for that new fat ass colonel."

We gulped. The colonel reddened and grabbed the intercom box, yelling, "Do you know who this is?"

The voice said, "Nope."

"This is the Colonel speaking."

There was dead silence. After several long seconds had elapsed, the voice said, "D-do you know who this is, sir?"

"No, I do not."

"Well then, so long, fat ass."

Communication is the key to relationships. Many bestsellers today point out that communication is affected by gender, a subject way beyond the scope of this book, but one for which I naturally have an opinion.

Who's a better communicator, a man or a woman? Women are better, but if you are a guy like me, it's not our fault. I'm going to let men off the hook here. You see, men and women are built differently. I don't mean in the obvious way, but insofar as our brains have two sides. The left side is task oriented, testosterone driven, wanting to get things done. The right side is creative and patient. All people have both sides. But women, because of differences in their physiological makeup, can communicate back and forth between the two sides a lot better than men can. Women have an eight-lane super highway between the two sides. Guys have a dirt path.

24,000 Words

A woman on any given day will use twenty-four thousand words to express herself. A man will use eleven thousand words a day. One of the problems we have in dual-career households in America today is that we both go do our thing all day long. By the time we get back home, the guy has seven words left. The woman has nine thousand. She comes home and says, "Hi, how was your day? Wait until I tell you about mine. We got last quarter's figures and we beat the quarter before and the quarter before that. You know that girl that works at the Y? It doesn't matter; she's pregnant. She changed her hair color. And your mother called to say we are invited to go on vacation the second week of August. How was your day?"

He stares at her, glassy-eyed and then says, "Food. Slippers. Beer. Remote. Sex. Happy. Sleep."

I want to thank you for reading my book. I hope you had as much fun as I had putting it together. Until we meet again, you have my very best wishes for success and good health in both your personal and professional lives.

In summary . . .

- *Communication is the key to good relationships.*

To laugh often and much; to win the respect of intelligent people and the affection of children; to earn the appreciation of honest critics and endure the betrayal of false friends; to appreciate beauty; to find the best in others; to leave this world a bit better, whether by a healthy child, a garden patch or a redeemed social condition; to know even one life has breathed easier because you have lived. This is to have succeeded.

—Ralph Waldo Emerson